From Your Friends at The MAILBOX®

The Earth

Grades 4–6

INVESTIGATING SCIENCE

Project Manager:
Elizabeth H. Lindsay

Writers:
Marcia Barton, Beth Gress, Linda Manwiller,
Kathleen Scavone, Patricia Twohey

Editors:
Cayce Guiliano, Peggy W. Hambright, Deborah T. Kalwat,
Scott Lyons, Jennifer Munnerlyn

Art Coordinator:
Clevell Harris

Artists:
Nick Greenwood, Clevell Harris,
Rob Mayworth, Greg D. Rieves

Cover Artists:
Nick Greenwood and Kimberly Richard

www.themailbox.com

©2000 by THE EDUCATION CENTER, INC.
All rights reserved.
ISBN #1-56234-412-9

Manufactured in the United States

10 9 8 7 6 5 4 3 2 1

Table of Contents

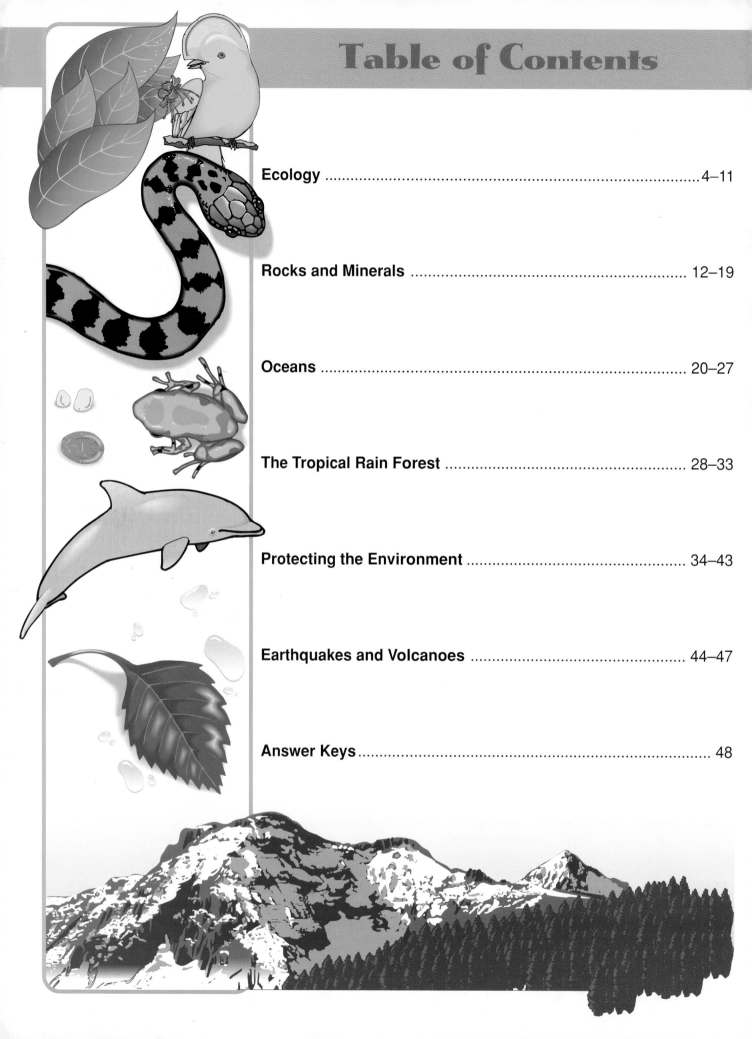

About This Book

Welcome to *Investigating Science—The Earth*! This book is one of eight must-have resource books that support the National Science Education Standards and are designed to supplement and enhance your existing science curriculum. Packed with practical cross-curricular ideas and thought-provoking reproducibles, these all-new, content-specific resource books provide intermediate teachers with a collection of innovative and fun activities for teaching thematic science units.

Included in this book:

Investigating Science—The Earth contains six cross-curricular thematic units, each containing

- Background information for the teacher
- Easy-to-implement instructions for science experiments and projects
- Student-centered activities and reproducibles
- Literature links

Cross-curricular thematic units found in this book:

- *Ecology*
- *Rocks and Minerals*
- *Oceans*
- *The Tropical Rain Forest*
- *Protecting the Environment*
- *Earthquakes and Volcanoes*

Other books in the intermediate Investigating Science series:

- *Investigating Science—Animals*
- *Investigating Science—Weather & Climate*
- *Investigating Science—Plants*
- *Investigating Science—Space*
- *Investigating Science—The Human Body*
- *Investigating Science—Light & Sound*
- *Investigating Science—Energy, Magnetism, & Machines*

Ecology

Help students understand that the earth is home to all kinds of organisms with the following creative activities and reproducibles.

Ecology Through the Alphabet
(Vocabulary, Art)

Background for the Teacher

- *Ecology* is the study of living things and how they behave and affect one another in their natural environment. It includes studying the consequences that can occur if any part of the relationship between a living thing and the earth is changed or destroyed.
- An *ecologist* is a person who studies living things and their environment.
- *Organisms* are living things, including people, animals, plants, bacteria, and fungi.
- Organisms can be classified as *producers, consumers,* or *decomposers.*
- Producers are plants that can produce their own food. Consumers are animals that must eat other organisms because they cannot produce their own food. Decomposers are organisms such as bacteria and fungi that feed on dead plants and animals and cause them to decay.
- An *ecosystem* consists of all the living and nonliving things in a given community. It can include many habitats and different kinds of living things. It can be as small as a puddle of water or as large as an ocean.
- A *community* is the plants and animals within a given habitat.
- A *habitat* is the actual place, such as a tree or desert, where an animal or plant lives.
- *Homeostasis* is the balance in the number of plants and animals in an ecosystem.

Use this picture-perfect activity to show students that learning ecological vocabulary is as easy as their ABCs! First, discuss with students the definition of *ecology* (see the background information on this page). Next, give each student a sheet of drawing paper and assign him a different word from the list below. If desired, replace any word with one of your own or of students' choosing, or use one of the words in parentheses instead. Direct the student to copy the assigned word onto his paper and define it (using a reference book, if necessary). Have him add an illustration and a sentence showing how the word relates to ecology. After students have shared their work with the class, have each child decorate a picture frame on a larger sheet of light-colored construction paper, cut it out, and then tape it to his paper. Then display the papers in alphabetical order on a bulletin board. Or combine the papers into a class booklet students can use for a quick review.

A—abiotic (acid rain, adaptation)	**M**—marine life (microorganisms)
B—biome (bacteria, biodegradable, biotic)	**N**—niche
C—community (carnivores, conserve, consumers)	**O**—omnivores (ocean, organisms)
D—decomposers (desert)	**P**—producers (pond, predator)
E—ecologist (ecosystem, environment, estuary)	**Q**—quail
F—food chain (food web, forest, fungi)	**R**—river (recycle)
G—grassland	**S**—species (savanna)
H—habitat (herbivores, homeostasis)	**T**—top consumer (taiga, tundra)
I—insects	**U**—umbrella tree
J—jellyfish	**V**—vegetation
K—kangaroo	**W**—wetland (water cycle)
L—lake (landfill, leachate)	**X**—extinction
	Y—yak
	Z—zebra (zoology)

Eco-Expert Books

Ecology (Usborne Science & Experiments series) by Richard Spurgeon (EDC Publications, 1990)

Janice VanCleave's Ecology for Every Kid: Easy Activities That Make Learning Science Fun (John Wiley & Sons, Inc.; 1996)

The Missing 'Gator of Gumbo Limbo: An Ecological Mystery by Jean Craighead George (HarperTrophy, 1993)

Food Chain—a series of living things linked together in the order in which they feed on each other.

If something happens to one part of a food chain, it affects the other links, too.

Fascinating Food Chains
(Making Models, Making Connections, Drawing Conclusions)

Help students understand the important connections of producers, consumers, and decomposers with this cooperative activity. First, review with students that a *food chain* is a series of organisms linked according to the *order* in which they feed on one another. For example, explain that a green plant (a producer) gets eaten by a first-order consumer (an animal that eats plants, called an *herbivore*). That animal can get eaten by a second-order consumer (an animal that eats animals, called a *carnivore*). That animal can get eaten by a third-order consumer (another carnivore). The animal at the top of a food chain (last in the order) is the *top consumer*. When the top consumer dies, it decomposes by having decomposers (bacteria and fungi) feed on it.

Next, divide students into groups of three. Assign each group one of the food chains from those suggested below. Or challenge each group to create its own. Give the groups the materials needed (see the list) and then guide them through the steps provided to create their food chain models.

After each group shares its completed food chain with the class, have two groups place their chains on the floor. Have the members of those groups look for common links in the two chains that can be joined. For example, a hawk eats both rabbits and squirrels. So a group having a hawk linked to a rabbit can join its hawk to another group's squirrel. Continue by having one group at a time join its chain to one on the floor to create a food web of as many connections as possible. When every group has found a place to add its chain, have students survey the completed web. Then ask questions that help students understand how a change in one link can affect another, such as "What would happen if there were no hawks to eat the rabbits?" Finally, display the web on a wall titled "What a Wonderful (Food) Web We Weave!" To extend the activity, challenge students to classify the display's consumers into herbivores, carnivores, and *omnivores* (eaters of both plants and animals).

Materials for each group:
magazines
scissors
glue
crayons or markers
access to a hole puncher
two to four 5" lengths of yarn
    (depending on chain
    created), plus extras for
    making web connections
construction paper circles:
    1 green, 2 to 4 red
    (depending on chain
    created), and 1 brown

Steps:
1. On the green circle, draw and label a picture of a green plant. Or cut out a magazine picture of a plant and glue it on the circle.
2. On one red circle, draw and label or cut out an animal (a first-order consumer) that could eat the plant shown on the green circle.
3. On another red circle, draw and label or cut out an animal (a second-order consumer) that could eat the animal on the first red circle.
4. On the third red circle (if being used), draw and label or cut out an animal (a third-order consumer) that could eat the animal shown on either the first or second red circles. Do the same with the fourth red circle, drawing and labeling an animal that could eat the one shown on the first, second, or third red circles.
5. On the brown circle, draw and label bacteria or fungi (the decomposers) that help animals decay when they die.
6. Use a hole puncher and yarn to connect the circles in the order that they were made.

Food Chains

Producer	First-Order Consumer	Second-Order Consumer	Third-Order Consumer	"Top" Consumer	Decomposer
clover	rabbit	fox			bacteria and fungi
grass	rabbit	hawk			bacteria and fungi
leaves	cricket	mouse	owl		bacteria and fungi
leaves	cricket	frog	baby raccoon	hawk	bacteria and fungi
clover	grasshopper	bird	fox		bacteria and fungi
leaves	grasshopper	frog	snake	hawk	bacteria and fungi
grass	deer	wolf			bacteria and fungi
corn	mouse	fox			bacteria and fungi
acorn	mouse	weasel	fox		bacteria and fungi
acorn	squirrel	fox			bacteria and fungi
seeds	chipmunk	hawk			bacteria and fungi

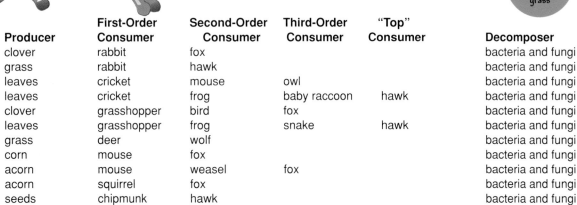

Building Box Biomes
(Research, Making a Model)

Sharpen students' research skills with a project that focuses on major land and water biomes. First, share with students that a *biome* is a plant and animal community that covers a large geographic area. Next, assign each pair of students a different biome from the lists below. Direct the pair to research the climate, geographic features, and plants and animals of its assigned biome, plus one or more places where that biome can be found. Then have the pair decorate a shoebox using a variety of materials—such as magazine cutouts, plastic figures, grass, rocks, and twigs—to create a diorama showing the specific features of that biome. When the projects have been completed, have each pair present its project to the class, pointing out on a world map the places where that biome can be found. If desired, follow up the activity by displaying the projects on a table and having each student write a paragraph comparing any two of the biomes.

Land Biomes
Tundra
Taiga
Temperate Coniferous Forest
Temperate Deciduous Forest
Chaparral
Desert
Grassland
Savanna
Tropical Rain Forest
Tropical Seasonal Forest

Aquatic Biomes
Ponds and Lakes
Streams and Rivers
Wetlands
Oceans
Coral Reefs
Estuaries

Habitat in Hand
(Observing, Describing, Writing)

Help students get better acquainted with plant and animal habitats by completing a project that takes them outdoors. First, review with students that a *habitat* is a place that provides any plant or animal with food, water, shelter, and space to live. Next, take the class outside where your young ecologists can spread out and find an ant, a butterfly, a squirrel, a bird, etc., in a small area to observe for about 15 minutes. Direct each observer to take notes about the major elements of the animal's habitat (food, water, shelter, space), plus its activity in that area.

After returning to the classroom, give each student a copy of the pattern on page 9, colored pencils, and scissors. Have the student use her notes to fill in the information on the pattern, including any clues related to human influences (either positive or negative). Have her add colored-pencil illustrations to the pattern (one per finger as shown) before cutting it out. After students share their observations with the class, display the cutouts on a wall to remind them that the care of the earth is in their hands!

Everything's Comin' Up...Bubbles!
(Demonstration)

Show students how important producers (green plants) are to preserving life on Earth with this oxygen-producing demonstration. Gather a few small bunches of aquatic plants (available at a tropical fish store), a glass mayonnaise or pickle jar, and a 2½-gallon aquarium. Place the aquarium in a sunny place and fill it three-fourths full of water. Submerge the jar in the aquarium, allowing the jar to fill completely with water and have no air bubbles. Next, put the plants inside the jar, again making sure there are no air bubbles in the jar. Then stand the jar upside down on the bottom of the aquarium. Over the next several days, let students observe what happens. *(Over a period of four to five days, bubbles of oxygen will slowly rise to the top of the inverted jar and create a small pocket of air.)*

If desired, follow up the demonstration by having students brainstorm other benefits of green plants as you list them on the board (see the list shown). Then have each student write a sentence and draw an illustration summarizing one of the benefits on a blue construction paper circle. Display the cutouts on a bulletin board titled "Green Plants: Bubbling Over With Benefits!"

Benefits of Green Plants
- Food, such as fruits and vegetables
- Clothing from cotton plants
- Lumber for houses and furniture
- Medicines, such as antibiotics and pain relievers
- Wood for fuel
- Paper and paper products from trees
- Pleasure from beautiful gardens and flowers
- Conservation of soil from roots holding soil

Decomposers at Work
(Demonstration, Making Observations, Writing Poetry)

Introduce students to the least familiar members of the food chain—the decomposers—by having them study the changes that occur within a mold terrarium. First, gather a clean, clear glass (or plastic) quart-sized jar with a screw-on lid; a few small food scraps, such as bread, fresh fruit or vegetables, and cheese (no meat or fish); masking tape; and one small cloth hand towel. If desired, ask students to contribute the items. Next, review with students that decomposers are organisms, such as bacteria and fungi, that feed on dead plants and animals. Explain that decomposers digest dead matter, breaking it down into substances that enrich the soil and help green plants grow. Next, have students watch what you do, explaining that you are going to construct a habitat for decomposers. Put the food scraps inside the jar and tighten the lid. Wrap the area between the lid and the jar with masking tape. Fold the towel and place the jar on its side, atop the folded towel (to keep the jar from rolling). Then give each student a copy of page 10 to use for recording what happens *(contents will gradually decompose, some showing evidence of mold growth)*. If desired, when the last observation has been made, have each student write a rhyming tribute with illustrations to these hardworking decomposers!

Discriminating Diets
(Critical Thinking, Creating a Menu)

If decomposers could dine at a restaurant, what would they want to see listed on a menu? Use this activity to help students answer that question! First, review with students that the role of decomposers is to break down the remains of plants and animals into substances that are helpful to the environment. Next, make two columns on the board, one labeled "Biodegradable" and the other "Nonbiodegradable." Discuss with students the difference between these two terms *(biodegradable—able to be broken down naturally by bacteria or fungi; nonbiodegradable—not able to be broken down by bacteria or fungi).* Then call out one item at a time from the list below for students to discuss and list on the board under the corresponding category.

Finally, give each student a sheet of colorful construction paper and crayons or markers. Have her use the materials to design a classy dinner menu consisting of biodegradable items that would appeal to the discriminating tastes of decomposers. Display students' creations on a bulletin board titled "Menus That Whet Decomposers' Appetites!" For an interesting follow-up project that students can complete at home to observe how substances decompose over a period of time, see the activity on page 11.

Decomposers' Delights

Appetizers
apple slices
crackers
strawberries

Main Courses
bread
cloth
paper
craft stick

Desserts
candy
cake

biodegradable	nonbiodegradable
paper	Styrofoam®
cloth	plastic toy
apple slice	disposable pen
craft stick	paper clip
hard candy	pencil (metal part, lead, eraser)
cracker	disposable diaper (plastic liner)
bread	
cake	
pencil (wood)	
disposable diaper (paper part)	

More Elbow Room, Please!
(Experiment, Writing, Critical Thinking)

By the year 2015, the United Nations estimates that the world's population will be 7.2 billion. Help students understand the effects of overcrowding with this simple experiment with plants described below. Follow up by having students discuss what happens. Then ask students to think of resources needed or desired by people (food, water, housing, products, etc.) and how an increase in the number of people living in an area could begin to affect the price, quantity, quality, and availability of those resources. Finally, challenge students to suggest solutions to the problems that could arise due to overcrowded conditions.

Materials:
five 3" clay (or plastic) pots with saucers
potting soil
self-stick labels
black marker
water
tablespoon
51 seeds, such as bean or tomato

Steps:
1. Label the pots with numbers from 1 to 5. Fill each pot with potting soil.
2. Plant 1 seed in Pot 1, 5 seeds in Pot 2, 10 seeds in Pot 3, 15 seeds in Pot 4, and 20 seeds in Pot 5. On the corresponding labels, record the number of seeds planted in each pot.
3. Place the pots in a sunny location. Add water to moisten the soil. Water the plants as needed.
4. Have students monitor the seeds' growth every other day for two to three weeks. Direct each student to record his observations in a journal, relating how the plants compete for light, water, and nutrients. If desired, have him include illustrations of the plants.
5. After about two to three weeks, have each student write a paragraph comparing the condition and overall appearance of the plants in the pots *(not all of the seeds in Pots 2–5 may germinate, and the ones that do may begin to look scraggly and less healthy).*

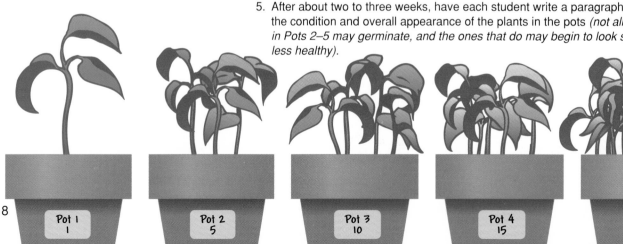

Pot 1 — 1
Pot 2 — 5
Pot 3 — 10
Pot 4 — 15
Pot 5 — 20

A _____'s
Habitat

Description: _____
_____
_____
_____
_____
_____
_____
_____

©2000 The Education Center, Inc. • *Investigating Science* • *The Earth* • TEC1734

Nature's Waste Patrol Team

Can you believe it? Mother Nature has been in the recycling business longer than humans! The members of her waste patrol team—bacteria and fungi—work to decompose plants and animals after they die, turning their remains into substances that enrich the soil. Follow the directions below to record the work of this hardworking group of recyclers.

Directions:

1. On the lines provided, list the foods your teacher placed inside the jar.
2. Observe the contents of the jar every other day (Monday, Wednesday, Friday) for two weeks.
3. In the chart, record the date of each observation and describe (or sketch) the scraps' appearance.
4. After finishing the last observation, answer the questions below.

Food Items Inside the Jar:

_____

_____

_____

_____

_____

Observations:

Date: _____	Date: _____	Date: _____
Date: _____	Date: _____	Date: _____

Questions:

1. How could you tell that decomposition was taking place? _____

_____

2. How do you think the decomposers got into the jar? _____

_____

3. If the scraps were to remain in the jar for two more weeks, how do you think they would look? _____

_____

Bonus Box: Use an encyclopedia to find out what Sir Alexander Fleming, a British bacteriologist, learned about one lifesaving decomposer. On the back of this page, write a sentence about this important discovery.

©2000 The Education Center, Inc. • *Investigating Science* • *The Earth* • TEC1734 • Key p. 48

10   **Note to the teacher:** Use with "Decomposers at Work" on page 7. Make one copy of this sheet for each student.

What's on the Menu?

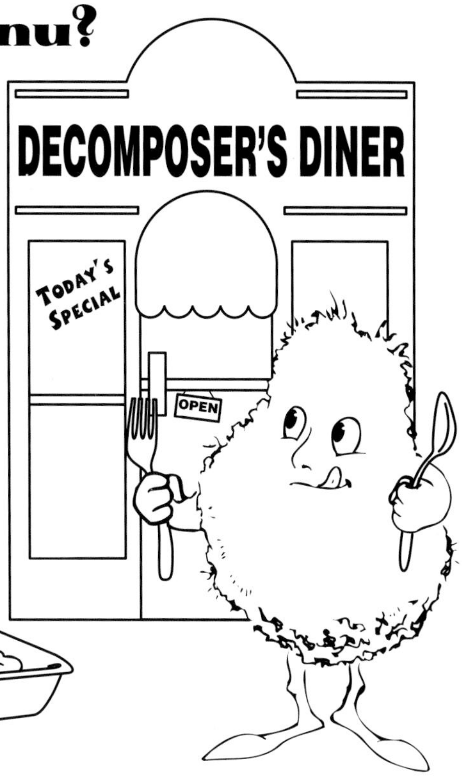

On what do decomposers such as bacteria and fungi like to dine? They prefer materials that are *biodegradable,* meaning ones that can be broken down into substances that do not harm the environment. Materials that cannot be broken down are *non-biodegradable.* Follow the steps below to find out what such picky-eating decomposers would want on their dinner menus!

Materials for each group of students:

13" x 9" aluminum pan filled with about 2 1/2" soil (not commercial)
6 different test items, such as paper, cloth, apple slice, Styrofoam®, small plastic toy, craft stick, hard candy, cracker or bread, small piece of cake, pencil, disposable pen, paper clip, plastic grocery bag square, or disposable diaper square
6 craft sticks
black marker
two 12" lengths of yarn
one 15" length of yarn
tape
water

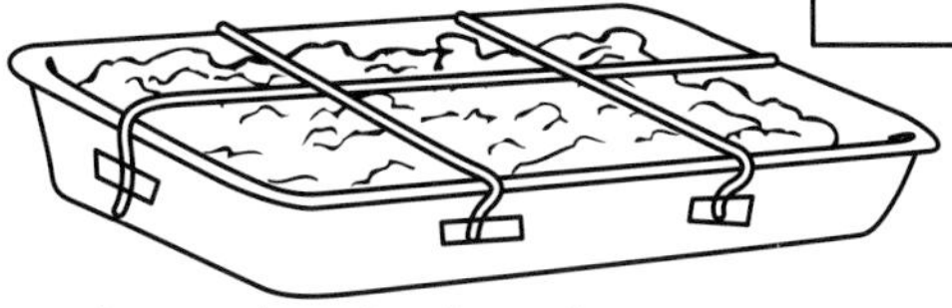

Steps for each student:

1. Divide the pan into six equal sections by taping the lengths of yarn to the edges of the pan as shown.
2. Using the marker, write the name of each test item on the end of a different craft stick.
3. Bury one test item at a time in a different section of soil. Then stand the corresponding craft stick upright in that section of soil to mark its place. When all the items have been buried and marked, moisten the soil with water.
4. On the lines provided below, predict which items you think will decompose.
5. Once each week, use the unlabeled end of the stick to carefully dig up each item. In the chart, note any changes in the items from the week before. Then rebury the items, adding water as needed to keep the soil moist.
6. After Week 4, answer the questions below. Write your answers on the back of this page or on another sheet of paper.

I think the following test items will show signs of decomposition: ____________________

____

Observations:

Week 1:	**Week 2:**
Week 3:	**Week 4:**

Questions:

1. Which of the items you buried could become part of a decomposer's diet? How do you know?
2. Which of the items you buried could *not* become part of a decomposer's diet? Why?

Note to the teacher: Use with "Discriminating Diets" on page 8.

Rocks and Minerals

Dig in to your study of rocks and minerals with this rockin' collection of activities and reproducibles!

Background for the Teacher

- A *mineral* is defined as any substance that is found in nature, has the same chemical makeup wherever it is found, has atoms that are arranged in a regular pattern and form solid units, and that, in most cases, is made up of substances that were never alive.
- *Rocks* are the solid parts of the earth. Most rocks are *aggregates,* or combinations, of one or more minerals. There are three main types of rocks: *igneous, sedimentary,* and *metamorphic.*
- *Igneous rocks* are made out of molten volcanic material that cools and hardens. The two main groups of igneous rocks are *extrusive rocks,* or rocks formed when magma is forced out onto the earth's surface, and *intrusive rocks,* or rocks formed when magma remains below the earth's surface.
- *Sedimentary rocks* are made from dead plant and animal matter. These layers become cemented together over time.
- *Metamorphic rocks* are formed from igneous and sedimentary rocks that have been put under extreme heat and pressure.
- The eight major characteristics used to identify and classify rocks are the following: *hardness* (ranging from softest to hardest), *color, streak* (the color that results when a rock is rubbed against something), *texture* (the size of the grains or crystals in the rock), *luster* (how a rock reflects light), *cleavage* (how a rock breaks), *chemical* (the chemical composition of a rock), and *density* (the amount of matter in a unit volume of any substance).
- *Gem minerals* are natural materials that are made into gemstones for jewelry.

I'd Like to Make a Deposit!
(Deposition Experiment)

Help your students understand how soil is deposited into layers with an activity you can bank on. Divide students into groups of four or five. Give each group a jar with a lid, and then take students outdoors and have each group gather enough rocky soil to fill its jar half full. Once back inside the classroom, direct each group to fill the rest of its jar with water and then screw the lid on tight. Instruct one group member to shake the jar, mixing the soil sample and the water (Figure 1). Then have each group draw an illustration of its jar and contents on a sheet of paper. Wait several days for the mixtures to settle, and then direct each group to draw a new illustration showing what has happened to the contents of its jar (Figure 2). *(Students should observe that the mixture has settled in layers.)* Follow up by discussing with students the process of *deposition,* the settling of materials carried by the agents of erosion (such as wind, water, and ice).

Figure 1   Figure 2

One Rockin' Booklist

The Best Book of Fossils, Rocks, and Minerals by Chris Pellant (Kingfisher, 2000)

Janice VanCleave's Rocks and Minerals: Mind-Boggling Experiments You Can Turn Into Science Fair Projects by Janice VanCleave (John Wiley & Sons, Inc.; 1996)

Let's Go Rock Collecting (Let's-Read-and-Find-Out Science® series) by Roma Gans (HarperCollins Publishers, Inc.; 1997)

Rocks and Minerals (National Audubon Society First Field Guide series) by Edward Ricciuti (Scholastic Inc., 1998)

Rock Slide Study Guide
(Making a Hands-On Study Guide)

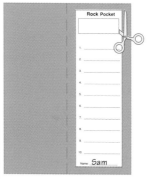

Figure 1

Figure 2

Slide into your study of rocks and minerals by having your students create a handy vocabulary study guide. First, choose ten vocabulary words such as those found in the background information on page 12. Write the words on a sheet of chart paper or a chalkboard along with a random listing of matching definitions. (Or, if desired, program a copy of the rock slide on page 16 with the definitions before duplicating and distributing to students.) Next, give each student the materials listed below and then guide students in completing the steps that follow. After each student has completed her study guide, check students' answers together as a class. Create new vocabulary lists and make additional copies of page 16 for your students to use throughout their studies.

Materials for each student: one 6" x 9" sheet of colorful construction paper, 1 copy of page 16, scissors, glue, tape

Figure 3

Figure 4

Steps:

1. Cut out the rock pocket and rock slide on page 16. Write your name on each cutout. (Figure 1)
2. Fold the piece of construction paper in half lengthwise; then glue the rock pocket to one side. (Figure 2)
3. Unfold the construction paper and cut out the window (rock pocket and construction paper) at the top of the rock pocket. (Figure 3)
4. Refold the construction paper, taping the right edges together. Do not tape the top or bottom. (Figure 4)
5. Write the definitions from the list your teacher gives you on your rock slide. Insert the slide into the construction-paper pocket, sliding it until the first definition can be seen in the window. (Figure 5)
6. On line 1 of the rock pocket, write the vocabulary word from the list that matches the first definition. (Figure 6) Use reference materials for help, if necessary.
7. Continue until you match one vocabulary word for each definition. (Figure 7)

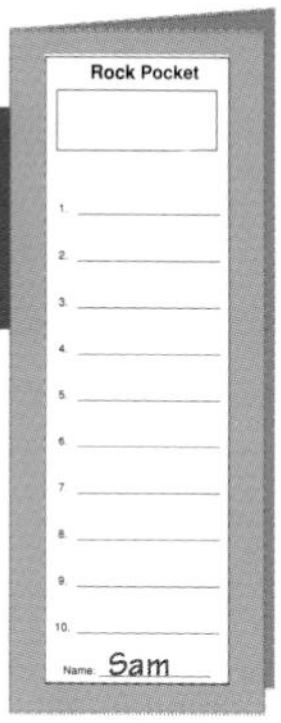

Figure 5

Figure 6

Figure 7

Name That Rock!
(Research, Rock Identification)

Watch your students become rock sleuths as they gather clues to help them identify different types of rocks. In advance, create a Mystery Rock Box by covering a shoebox with construction paper and gluing small pebbles to the sides and top as shown. Also gather a collection of the rocks on the chart shown at the left (most are available through catalogs such as Carolina Biological Supply®). Or gather rock types of your own choosing and adjust the chart as necessary. Display the rock chart on a chalkboard or an overhead transparency. Have each student copy the chart onto a sheet of paper and then use reference materials to help him complete the missing information. Afterward, check students' answers together as a class.

Place one rock inside the box. Then direct a student volunteer to use his chart to ask a yes-or-no question about the mystery rock, such as "Is the rock metamorphic?" or "Is it green?" After asking a question, allow that student to guess the type of rock. Continue in the same manner until a student discovers its identity. Once the mystery rock has been named, allow the student who correctly identified it to choose the next rock to go in the box and answer classmates' questions.

Rock Chart			
Name	Type	Texture	Color
Granite	igneous	medium to coarse crystals	white, gray, pink, red
Shale			
Obsidian			
Schist			
Chalk			
Slate			
Gneiss			
Basalt			
Sandstone			
Pumice			
Marble			
Limestone			

Rock Wall
(Research, Classifying)

Your students will be climbing the walls to complete this rock-classifying activity! First, pair students and give each pair a plastic grocery bag. Take students outside, directing them to gather in their bags as many *different* rocks as possible. Once back inside the classroom, provide pairs access to appropriate reference materials to help them identify each rock found. Then, as a class, make a list of all the different rocks collected. Next, assign each pair a rock from the above-mentioned list and give partners an 8" x 8" sheet of light-colored tagboard, a plain 5" x 8" index card, crayons or markers, and glue. Instruct the pair to research its rock for information such as mineral composition, characteristics (see the background information on page 12), and environment. Then have the pair detail its research by writing on the index card a descriptive paragraph and including an accompanying labeled illustration. Direct the pair to glue its rock and index card on the tagboard. Finally, with students' help, create a "Rock Wall" bulletin board, as shown, on which to display their work.

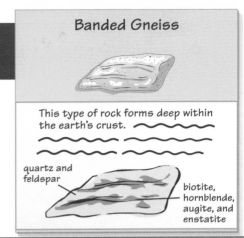

Banded Gneiss

This type of rock forms deep within the earth's crust.

quartz and feldspar

biotite, hornblende, augite, and enstatite

ROCK WALL

Rock-Type Road Maps
(Creating a Map, Art)

Name Rachel
Rock-Type Road Map
United States

Key
Igneous
(rock made from molten volcanic material)
Sedimentary
(rock made from dead plant and animal matter)
Metamorphic
(rock made from sedimentary and igneous rocks)

Put your students on the right road to studying U.S. rock locations with this colorful, hands-on map activity. Before beginning the activity, remind students that there are three main types of rocks: *igneous, sedimentary,* and *metamorphic.* Discuss how these rock types can be found in different areas of the United States (see the map on this page). Next, divide students into groups of three, providing each student with a copy of the map on page 17 and access to reference materials. Direct the group to research the areas in the United States in which each rock type can be found. Have each student create a key and then carefully mark each area on his map. Next, give each group the materials listed below. Then guide each group through the steps that follow.

Materials for each group: newspaper, 3 paper cups half full of sand, 3 different food colorings, 3 craft sticks, glue, toothpicks

Steps:
1. Cover your desk or table with newspaper.
2. Put about four drops of a different food coloring into each cup of sand. Use a craft stick to mix the sand in each cup to the desired color.
3. On the map key on page 17, put a small drop of glue in each box. Put a different color of sand in the glue on each box.
4. On your map, locate the areas in which igneous rocks can be found. Use a toothpick to put a small amount of glue on these areas. Then, using the key as a guide, add the corresponding colored sand to those areas.
5. Repeat Step 4 for the areas in which sedimentary and metamorphic rocks can be found.
6. Put your map aside until the glue has dried, and then gently blow off any excess sand.
7. Share your map with your classmates.

Metamorphic Marshmallows!
(Experiment)

Watch your students' opinions about studying rocks metamorphose as they complete this colorful experiment! Explain to students that igneous and sedimentary rocks can change to metamorphic rocks over long periods of time. This is caused by the extreme pressure and heat found deep within the earth. Further explain that this heat and pressure can cause the minerals from these rocks to move, be squeezed into new sizes and shapes, or become completely new minerals. Next, give each student about 20 small colored marshmallows and two six-inch square sheets of waxed paper. Then guide them in creating their own metamorphic rocks by following the steps below. Afterward, discuss what happened to the marshmallow pieces and how this is similar to the process igneous and sedimentary rocks go through in becoming metamorphic rocks. *(Students should observe that the marshmallow pieces stick together to make one mass. This is due to the pressure from being stepped on and from the heat of the sun, just as it is with igneous and sedimentary rocks becoming metamorphic rocks due to the extreme pressure and heat inside the earth.)*

Steps:
1. Place one sheet of waxed paper on your desk.
2. Tear the marshmallows (representing igneous and sedimentary rocks) into pieces. Place them in a pile on the waxed paper.
3. Cover the pile with the other sheet of waxed paper.
4. Carefully put the waxed papers and marshmallows on the floor. Press the marshmallows firmly together by stepping on the pile. (Figure 1)
5. Place the waxed papers and marshmallows outside in a sunny spot for about half an hour.
6. Observe the changes in the marshmallows. (Figure 2)

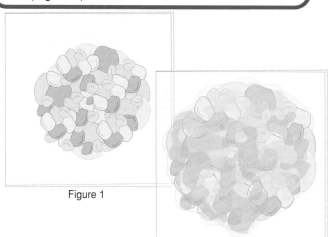

Figure 1

Figure 2

Q: What types of rocks become metamorphic rocks?
A: Sedimentary and igneous rocks become metamorphic rocks.

Q: How is coal formed?
A: Coal is formed when dense plant materials that have been buried for a long time and did not completely rot become compressed into rock made mostly of carbon.

The Lost City of "Gemtopia"
(Game)

Challenge your students to find out more about rocks as they work their way through this student-created game. Divide students into groups of four or five. Give each group the materials listed below and then guide them through the directions for assembling and playing the game.

Materials for each group: 1 copy of the gameboard on page 18, 1 set of Fate Cards on page 19, 12 index cards, 1 die, 1 rock (game piece) for each player, 1 black marker, crayons, reference books

Directions for assembling the game:
1. Color the gameboard on page 18. Place it on a playing surface.
2. Cut out the Fate Cards on page 19 and place them facedown next to the gameboard.
3. Label four index cards "Igneous," four "Sedimentary," and four "Metamorphic." Use the provided reference materials to help you write a question and corresponding answer about each type of rock on the back of the appropriate index cards.
4. Place the three sets of labeled cards facedown next to the gameboard.

Directions for playing the game:
1. All players place their rocks on the start space. Player 1 rolls the die and moves the number indicated.
2. If Player 1 lands on an I (igneous), S (sedimentary), or M (metamorphic) space, Player 2 reads a question from a card in the appropriate pile. If Player 1 answers correctly, the card is discarded and she gets to roll again. If she answers incorrectly, the card is placed back at the bottom of the appropriate pile and she remains in that space until her next turn. Player 2 then takes a turn.
3. If a player lands on an F space, she draws a Fate Card and follows the given directions. If a player lands on a Free Space, she does not have to answer a question and play proceeds to the next person.
4. Play continues until one player reaches "Gemtopia!"

Patterns

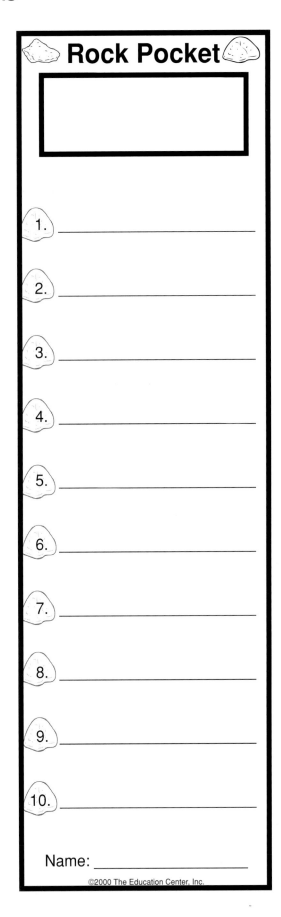

Rock Pocket

1. _____

2. _____

3. _____

4. _____

5. _____

6. _____

7. _____

8. _____

9. _____

10. _____

Name: _____

Rock Slide

1. _____
   _____

2. _____
   _____

3. _____
   _____

4. _____
   _____

5. _____
   _____

6. _____
   _____

7. _____
   _____

8. _____
   _____

9. _____
   _____

10. _____
   _____

Name: _____

Note to the teacher: Use with "Rock Slide Study Guide" on page 13.

Identifying rock locations, making a map

Rock-Type Road Maps

United States

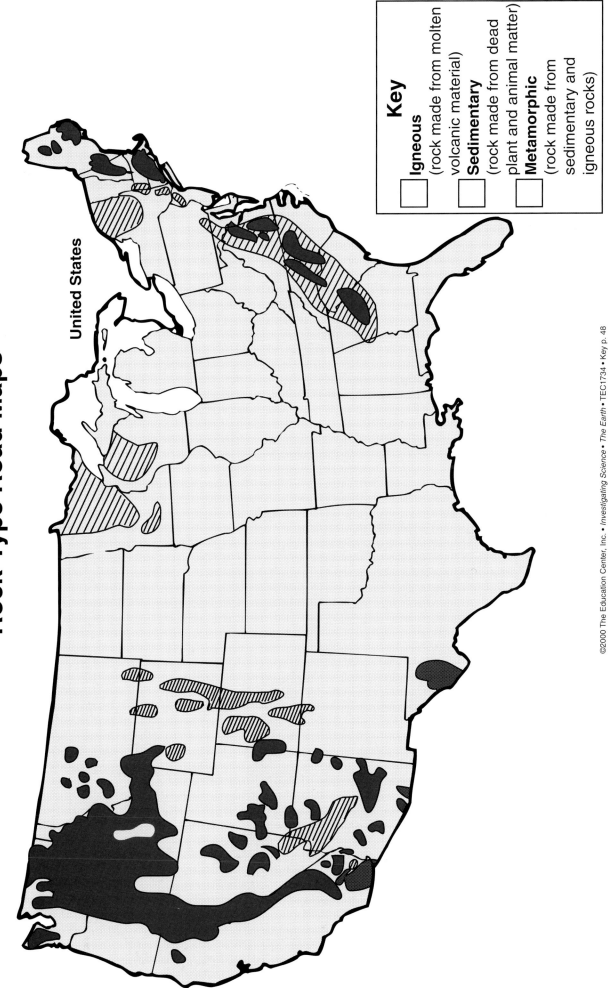

Key

Igneous
(rock made from molten volcanic material)

Sedimentary
(rock made from dead plant and animal matter)

Metamorphic
(rock made from sedimentary and igneous rocks)

Note to the teacher: Use with "Rock-Type Road Maps" on page 14.

The Lost City of "Gemtopia" Gameboard

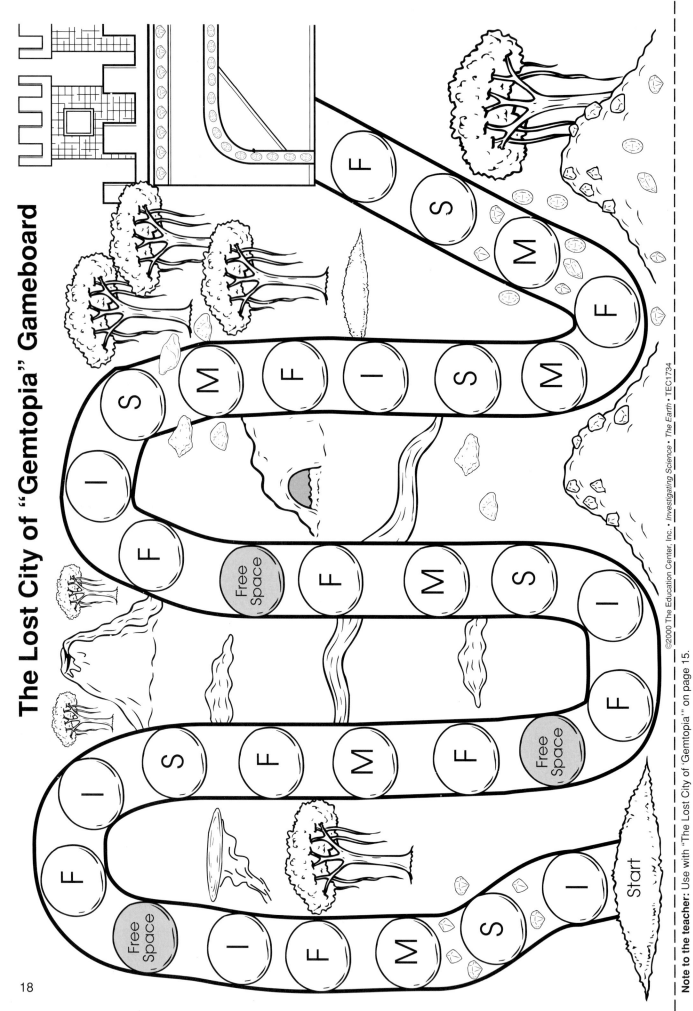

Note to the teacher: Use with "The Lost City of 'Gemtopia'" on page 15.

18

Fate Cards

Use with "The Lost City of 'Gemtopia'" on page 15.

You are stuck in a peat bog. **Your Fate:** lose 1 turn.

Rubies are scattered all around you and you stop to pick them up. **Your Fate:** lose 1 turn.

You find a secret tunnel! **Your Fate:** advance 2 spaces.

You find an extra flashlight to light your way! **Your Fate:** advance 1 space.

Molten lava is covering your path. **Your Fate:** go back 2 spaces.

You're stuck in quicksand. **Your Fate:** go back 3 spaces.

You find boots with special rock-climbing spikes! **Your Fate:** advance 4 spaces.

You find a fossil imprint of part of an old city map! **Your Fate:** advance 4 spaces.

You're caught in a rock slide and you're hurt. **Your Fate:** go back 3 spaces.

You notice something shiny on a hillside and stop to take a look. **Your Fate:** go back 2 spaces.

A vein of gold is leading you to the city! **Your Fate:** advance 6 spaces.

You make a raft out of pumice, the only rock that floats! **Your Fate:** advance 6 spaces.

Severe weather has caused the path to become too muddy to cross. **Your Fate:** go back 2 spaces.

You discover some emeralds and stop to look at them. **Your Fate:** lose 1 turn.

You notice diamonds up ahead! **Your Fate:** advance 5 spaces.

You swing safely across some molten rocks! **Your Fate:** advance 3 spaces.

Oceans

*Reel your students into studying the ocean
with the following activities that are
swimming with creativity!*

Background for the Teacher

- The oceans cover 71 percent of the earth's surface.
- The Pacific, Atlantic, Indian, and Arctic oceans make up the four large bodies of water separating the continents. The many seas, bays, and gulfs are actually part of these four oceans. (Some scientists actually consider the Arctic Ocean to be part of the Atlantic Ocean, and therefore call it the Arctic Sea.)
- The ocean can be divided into distinct layers or zones according to the amount of light each one receives: *the sunlight zone, the twilight zone,* and *the midnight zone.*
- The sunlight zone reaches depths from 0 to 600 feet and receives the most sunlight. The twilight zone ranges in depth from 600 to 3,000 feet and receives very little sunlight. The midnight zone depth ranges from 3,000 to about 15,000 feet. The only light in this zone is produced by *bioluminescence,* a process by which organisms produce their own light.
- An ocean is a complex ecosystem containing a vast number of plants and unusual creatures, ranging in size from microscopic organisms to the giant blue whale, each being specially adapted to live in its habitat.
- Ocean plants and plantlike creatures rely on sunlight and the minerals in the water to grow. In turn, various animals eat these organisms and one another.
- The ocean floor includes a variety of geographic features such as mountains, volcanoes, trenches, and valleys.
- The oceans provide a wealth of resources, including food, energy, minerals, and medicines.

Ocean Books to Hook Into

A Visual Introduction to Whales, Dolphins and Porpoises (Animal Watch series) by Bernard Stonehouse (Checkmark Books™, 1998)

Fearsome Fish (Creepy Creatures series) by Steve Parker (Raintree Steck-Vaughn Publishers, 1994)

I Didn't Know That Sharks Keep Losing Their Teeth and Other Amazing Facts About Sharks by Claire Llewellyn (Copper Beech Books, 1998)

Oceans (Saving Our World series) by Jane Parker (Copper Beech Books, 1999)

Saltwater Scenes
(Research, Art)

Dive into your study of the deep blue by having your class complete this beautiful ocean art project! Begin by explaining to your students that every natural element can be found in the ocean's waters, but it is mainly known for its salts. Further explain that many of these salts come from rocks on land. As the rocks break down, salts (and other materials) are carried to the ocean through rivers. While holding up a container of salt, point out to students that most of the ocean salt is a compound called *sodium chloride,* which is simply ordinary table salt. Distribute the materials below to each student, and then use the directions to guide them in creating their salty scenes.

Materials for each student: access to a variety of ocean reference materials (see the booklist on this page), two 9" x 12" sheets of white construction paper, blue and green watercolor paints, a paintbrush, a cup of water, salt, colored pencils or crayons, glue, scissors, a 10" x 13" sheet of plastic wrap, tape

Directions:
1. Paint a wet, watercolor wash over the entire sheet of construction paper using a mix of blue and green paint.
2. Immediately sprinkle a measure of salt over the paper. (You should see the salt begin dissolving in the water wash, creating a display of patterns or textures.)
3. While the paint is drying, use reference materials to help you draw and color a variety of ocean plants and animals on the other sheet of construction paper.
4. Carefully cut out the pictures and arrange them on the dried salt scene; then glue them in place.
5. Lay the scene facedown on the plastic wrap. Fold over the edges of the wrap, taping them to the back of the paper.

How Much of the Earth Is Covered by Water?
(Probability Experiment)

Plunge your students into the study of the world's oceans with this hands-on probability activity. Remind students that more than 70 percent of the earth is covered with water. Based on this fact, have students identify what percentage of the earth is covered by land *(less than 30%)*. Next, ask the class this question: if a blindfolded student were directed to touch his finger on any spot of the globe, what is the *probability* (chance or likelihood) he would touch water? Land? Help students recognize that because more than 70 percent of the earth is covered by water, the probability of touching water would be greater than touching land. Next, divide students into ten groups and give each group the materials listed below. Guide each group through the steps that follow. After each group completes ten trials, direct it to determine a percentage for the number of times the coordinates landed on water versus land. Survey each group and record its percentage on the chalkboard. Then calculate a class average. Have students compare the class average to the actual amount of the earth's surface covered by water.

Materials for each group: 1 sheet of loose-leaf paper, 1 enlarged copy of the latitude and longitude chart at the right, scissors, 2 resealable plastic bags, access to a globe

Steps:

1. Create a frequency table on a sheet of loose-leaf paper like the one shown.
2. Cut apart the strips on the chart. Place the latitude strips in one bag and the longitude strips in another. Label the bags accordingly.
3. Draw one latitude and one longitude strip from each bag. Read aloud the coordinates and locate the coordinates on a globe.
4. Mark a tally in the first column of the table according to where the coordinate landed. Return the strips to the bags.
5. Repeat Steps 3–4 nine more times, recording a tally in the appropriate row each time followed by the resulting frequency tallies.

Frequency Table

Area	Tally	Frequency
Land		
Water		

LATITUDES	LONGITUDES	LONGITUDES
90° N Latitude	0° Longitude	170° W Longitude
80° N Latitude	10° E Longitude	160° W Longitude
70° N Latitude	20° E Longitude	150° W Longitude
60° N Latitude	30° E Longitude	140° W Longitude
50° N Latitude	40° E Longitude	130° W Longitude
40° N Latitude	50° E Longitude	120° W Longitude
30° N Latitude	60° E Longitude	110° W Longitude
20° N Latitude	70° E Longitude	100° W Longitude
10° N Latitude	80° E Longitude	90° W Longitude
0° Latitude	90° E Longitude	80° W Longitude
10° S Latitude	100° E Longitude	70° W Longitude
20° S Latitude	110° E Longitude	60° W Longitude
30° S Latitude	120° E Longitude	50° W Longitude
40° S Latitude	130° E Longitude	40° W Longitude
50° S Latitude	140° E Longitude	30° W Longitude
60° S Latitude	150° E Longitude	20° W Longitude
70° S Latitude	160° E Longitude	10° W Longitude
80° S Latitude	170° E Longitude	
90° S Latitude	180° Longitude	

Under the Sea
(Identifying Life in the Ocean Zones)

Send your students diving into the depths of the sea with this student-centered bulletin board activity. First, horizontally overlap three different-colored sections of bulletin board paper on a bulletin board. Then, starting at the top, label each section accordingly: *Sunlight Zone, Twilight Zone,* and *Midnight Zone* (Figure 1). Next, use the background information on page 20 to discuss these three zones with students. Then divide students into groups of three or four. Provide each group with access to reference materials and give each group three 9" x 12" sheets of white construction paper. Have each group research one plant or animal for each zone.

For each plant or animal researched, direct the group to fold a sheet of construction paper in half and draw a picture of it along the fold (Figure 2). Have the group cut out its picture, being careful not to cut the fold line (Figure 3). On the inside of the cutout, have the group write the plant's or animal's name and several interesting facts about it. On the outside of the cutout, instruct the group to draw and color the organism's characteristics. If desired, encourage the group to use a variety of arts-and-crafts supplies to add detail to its drawing (Figure 4). Finally, have each group attach its plants and animals to the appropriate zones on the prepared bulletin board.

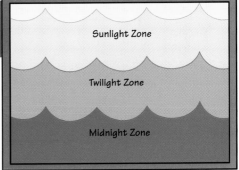

Figure 1

Figures 2–3

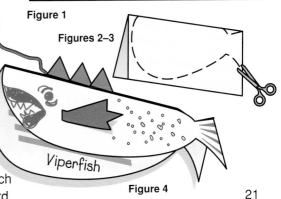

Viperfish

Figure 4

21

Sizin' Up the Seas
(Demonstration, Using a Scale, Making a Model)

Help your students size up the seas by creating a scale model of the four major oceans. First, explain to students that the oceans' waters form one great body often called the *world ocean.* The continents divide this one ocean into four smaller oceans, including the *Pacific,* the *Atlantic,* the *Indian,* and the *Arctic.* Display the chart below, discussing the relative size of each ocean. Remind students that when scientists make maps showing the sizes of the oceans, they use a *scale (unit of measure that compares an actual distance to a distance on a map or model).* Hold up a sheet of quarter-inch graph paper. Point out to students that there 945 squares on the grid *(27 x 35 grid).* Ask each student how many sheets of graph paper are needed to show the size of the Pacific Ocean using a scale of a quarter inch equals one square mile *(63,800,000 ÷ 945 = 67,514 sheets).* Lead students to understand that a larger scale is needed (quarter-inch square = 10,000 square miles). As a class, use this scale to find out how many quarter-inch squares and how many sheets of graph paper are needed to show the size of each ocean *(Pacific Ocean—6,380 squares, seven sheets; Atlantic Ocean—3,180 squares, four sheets; Indian Ocean—2,890 squares, four sheets; Arctic Ocean—540 squares, one sheet).*

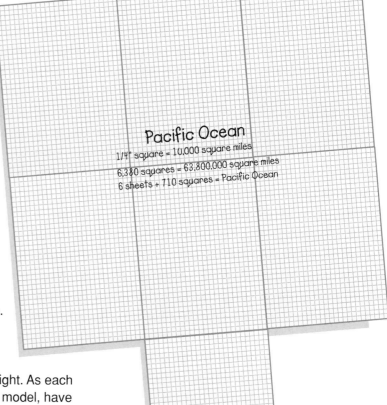

Pacific Ocean
1/4" square = 10,000 square miles
6,380 squares = 63,800,000 square miles
6 sheets + 710 squares = Pacific Ocean

Next, divide students into eight groups, assigning each group an ocean. Provide each group with the appropriate amount of graph paper, scissors, and tape. Direct the group to assemble its graph paper to create an accurate model of its ocean's size and label it as shown in the example at the right. As each group shares its model, have students compare and contrast the sizes of the oceans.

Ocean Areas in Square Miles	
Pacific	63,800,000
Atlantic	31,800,000
Indian	28,900,000
Arctic	5,400,000

Captivating Coral Reefs
(Research, Constructing a Model)

Plant or animal? Living or dead? These are the questions to ask when talking about coral reefs. Explain to students that the majority of a coral reef is made up of the skeletons of millions of dead coral animals with only the surface layer containing living coral animals. So, the answer to the questions above? Living *and* dead animals! Point out to students that there are three types of coral reefs—a *fringing reef* (extends from shore into the sea), a *barrier reef* (follows the shoreline, creating a barrier between the open sea and the water near the shoreline), and an *atoll* (contains a lagoon inside its circular structure). Next, divide students into small groups, assigning each group one type of coral reef. Provide each group with a shoebox and a variety of materials, such as pastas, cereals, yarn, pipe cleaners, pebbles, rice, sponges, and paint supplies. Direct each group to research its reef and then construct a model showing its unique structure. After the reefs are constructed, have each group share its reef and identify its unique features. Display the reef models in the school library to captivate other classes!

an atoll

Treasures From the Sea
(Research, Making Descriptive Observations)

Dig into this activity in which students search the sands for products from the sea! First, obtain an empty copy-paper box. Title the outside of the box "Treasures From the Sea." Then, with students' help, decorate it with shells and pictures of sea life as shown. Fill the bottom of the box with sand purchased from a home-supply store and place it in a special area of the room. Then share with students how the oceans provide a wealth of resources, including food, medicines, and other products. Post a sheet of chart paper near the treasure box. Have students research different products that come from the ocean (such as those shown in the illustration) and record their findings on the chart paper. Next, secretly assign each student a different item, instructing him to bring in to school the actual item or a picture cut out of a magazine. After students have had time to bring in their items or pictures, collect the items and bury them in the sand. Finally, choose one student to open the treasure box and dig up an item from the sand. (Direct the student to keep the item in the box so his classmates can't see it.) Instruct the student to use his senses (or his imagination if it is a picture) to help him describe the item—its texture, size, shape, color, etc. After each sensory description, have the student solicit guesses from his classmates. Allow the student that correctly guesses the item to then search for a treasure. Continue in this manner until each student has shared an item. If desired, follow up the activity by having each student write a descriptive paragraph about one of the items.

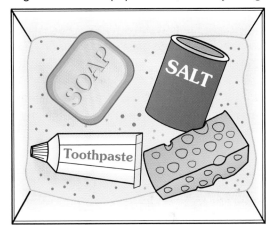

Fish Lengths

Type of Fish	Length in Feet
Atlantic Manta Ray	22
Blue Marlin	10
Bull Shark	8
Nassau Grouper	4
Trumpetfish	2
Green Moray Eel	6

0   5   10   15   20   25   30

Directions for making a graph:

1. Draw a horizontal and vertical axis on your paper. Label each axis.
2. Look at your data and determine what your scale should be. (Choose a scale with an appropriate interval. Be sure all of your bars will fit on the paper.)
3. Cut each length of yarn to match the appropriate length of each animal as shown on your graph.
4. Tape your yarn on the appropriate row on your graph.
5. Draw a picture of each animal beside its corresponding "bar."
6. Write a title for your graph.

Ocean Creatures Data Collection
(Data Collecting, Graphing)

Challenge your students to do a little data collecting about the crowd of marine creatures—minute and colossal—that inhabit the earth's oceans. First, share with students that the ocean's incredible variety of creatures range in size from microscopic organisms to giant blue whales. Then share with students the information in the sample graph shown. Remind them that graphs illustrate how data compare, and then point out the parts of the graph. Next, divide students into groups of three or four. Provide each group with a copy of the directions at the left, access to reference materials, a 12" x 18" sheet of light-colored construction paper, ten 18-inch lengths of colorful yarn, tape, scissors, and colored pencils or markers. Assign each group one of the animal groups listed below, directing the members to research ten different animals' sizes (or have each group choose ten creatures from different groups). Then have students display their data on a graph using the provided directions.

Ocean Animal Groups (Examples)

Fish (sharks, rays, tuna, cod)
Marine Reptiles (sea turtles, crocodiles)
Birds (puffins, gulls, pelicans)
Marine Mammals (whales, manatees, sea otters)

Coelenterata (jellyfish and sea anemones)
Mollusca (snails, squids, octopuses)
Arthropoda (crabs, shrimp, lobsters)
Echinoderms (sea stars, sea cucumbers, sea urchins)

Figure 1

Figure 2

Figure 3

My Whale Tale
by Lana

A Whale of a Tale
(Research, Creative Writing, Art)

Make a splash with this whale of a writing activity! Begin the activity by sharing with students that whales belong to a group of animals called *cetaceans* and that there are at least 75 different types of these creatures. Then read aloud a picture book about whales. Discuss with students the many characteristics that make whales unique, such as their tail *flukes* with distinct markings. Then brainstorm with students different types of whales. Invite each student to choose a type of whale to research. Instruct the student to list the characteristics that make her chosen whale unique.

Next, direct each student to write an imaginative story about her whale, being sure to incorporate the unique characteristics she discovered about it. To publish her story, give each student one 9" x 12" sheet of black construction paper, one sheet of loose-leaf paper, scissors, glue, and crayons. Have each student fold the construction paper in half, draw a fluke along the fold, and cut it out (Figure 1). Direct the student to draw distinguishing marks on her whale's tail using a white crayon (Figure 2). Next, instruct the student to cut along the top of her writing paper to resemble waves, color the waves, and then glue the bottom of her whale's tail to the back of it (Figure 3). Finally, direct the student to write the final draft of her story on her whale-tale writing paper. Display students' stories on a bulletin board titled "A Whale of a Tale."

Catchin' Ocean Words
(Vocabulary, Game)

Looking for just the right bait to get your students into studying their ocean vocabulary? Then this hands-on game is a "reel" catch! Choose 16 different ocean vocabulary words you wish your students to study. Write the words and corresponding definitions on a transparency or the chalkboard. (Or write the words and have students look up the definitions.) Then give each student a copy of the "Vocabulary Clue Catcher" on page 25, scissors, and tape. Guide students in following the directions below to assemble their clue catchers and play the game.

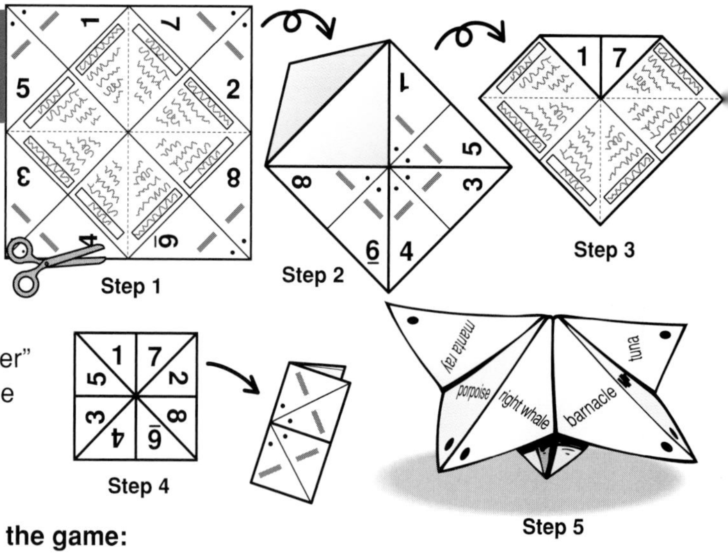

Step 1

Step 2

Step 3

Step 4

Step 5

To assemble the clue catcher:
1. Complete and cut out the patterns on page 25 as directed.
2. Place the square cutout facedown. Fold each corner of the square forward so that the points touch the center; then crease each fold along its edge.
3. Keeping each folded corner in place, flip the cutout over. Then fold each corner forward so that the points touch the dot in the center. Crease each fold along its edge.
4. Fold the resulting small square in half in one direction. Then unfold it and fold it in half in the other direction.
5. Place your thumbs and index fingers under the four flaps. Squeeze your thumbs and fingers together. Open and close the clue catcher by separating your fingers and thumbs first sideways and then back and forth.

To play the game:
1. Each player secretly chooses a vocabulary word from his clue catcher and lightly tapes his fishnet on it.
2. Player 1 begins the game by choosing an ocean animal on his opponent's clue catcher.
3. Player 2 opens and closes the catcher while spelling the animal's name.
4. Player 1 chooses a number from the opened catcher. Player 2 then lifts the flap and reads the definition under the chosen number. Player 1 identifies the vocabulary word that matches the definition. If answered correctly, he gets a point value equal to the number chosen. If answered incorrectly, no points are earned. If the player chooses a number with a fishnet beneath the flap and answers correctly, he earns double the point value.
5. Player 2 takes a turn in the same manner.
6. Play continues until all the numbers are chosen. The player with the most points at the end of the round wins. If desired, play several rounds, each time changing the placement of the fishnet before beginning.

Directions:
1. Cut out the large square and the fishnet along the bold lines.
2. Copy eight vocabulary words from the list your teacher gives you in each rectangle on the square cutout. Write each word's definition in the space below it.

Fishnet

Clue Catcher

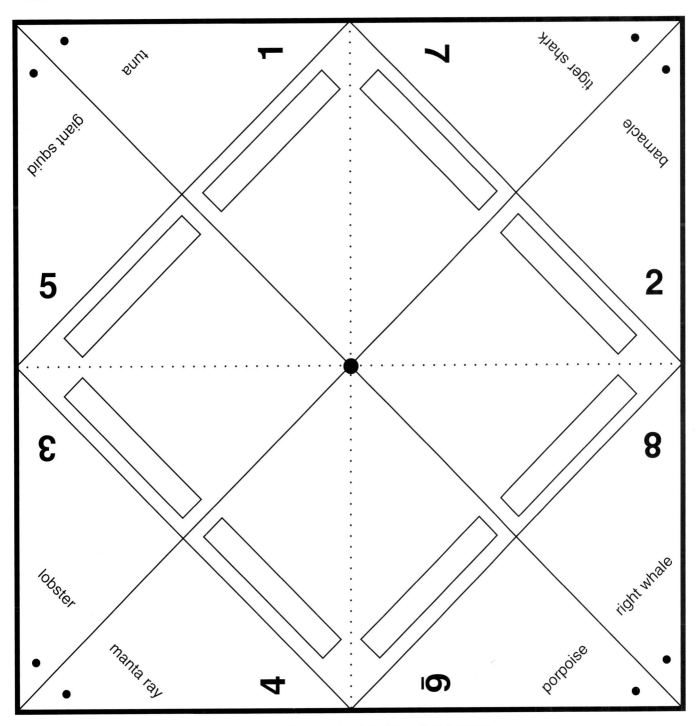

Note to the teacher: Use with "Catchin' Ocean Words" on page 24.

Identifying characteristics of sharks and dolphins

What's the Difference?

The Shark   The Dolphin

What is the difference between the shark and the dolphin? Plenty! Follow the directions below to find out more about these two unique ocean animals.

Directions:

1. Cut out the dashed rectangle, leaving the frame intact. Then cut apart the clue strips.
2. Color the frame, and then glue it to a 9" x 12" sheet of colorful construction paper.
3. Read each clue. Decide if it describes a shark or a dolphin and then arrange it on your paper under the correct heading.
4. Once you've arranged all of the strips, glue them on your paper.

- is a fish with a skeleton made of cartilage

- has a horizontal *caudal*, or tail, fin, which moves up and down to propel it through the water

- has a vertical *caudal*, or tail, fin, which moves from side to side to propel it through the water

- is extremely vocal, making rapid clicking noises to use as a form of sonar and high-pitched whistles to communicate

- often travels in groups called *herds*

- has several rows of sharp teeth, which are easily replaced when lost

- has skin that is sleek, smooth, and rubbery to the touch

- is covered with hard, sharp scales called *denticles*

- ranges from about four to nine feet in length

- is, like other whales, a mammal

- is *warm-blooded*, so it maintains a constant body temperature

- breathes through five to seven gill slits on each side

- breathes air through lungs and a blowhole at the top of its head

- sometimes attacks people and at other times leaves them alone

- is in most cases *cold-blooded*, so its body temperature changes with the surrounding water temperature

- sometimes gathers with others of its kind in a feeding frenzy

- has keen senses—sight, hearing, and smell—and can detect vibrations from great distances

- is a playful, sociable creature that has even been credited for saving drowning swimmers

- exhibits a high level of intelligence and can be trained to do tricks

- ranges from about six inches to 49 feet in length

©2000 The Education Center, Inc. • *Investigating Science • The Earth* • TEC1734 • Key p. 48

Note to the teacher: Provide each student with a 9" x 12" sheet of colorful construction paper; crayons or colored pencils; scissors; glue; and reference materials, if needed.

Name _____

Fish by the Thousands!

The world's ocean is just bubbling over with thousands of different kinds of fish—about 13,000 of them in fact! Follow the directions below to learn more about these spectacular species.

Directions:

1. Read each item in the bubbles below. Use the provided clues to help you match each fish to its corresponding description.
2. Check each pair by adding, subtracting, multiplying, or dividing the two numbers at the bottom of each bubble. (All correctly matched pairs equal 1,000.)
3. Then cut out the bubbles and glue each matching pair onto a sheet of colorful construction paper. Create an ocean scene by adding details to your paper, such as fish, seaweed, seashells, and other ocean life.

Sample

by Sammy

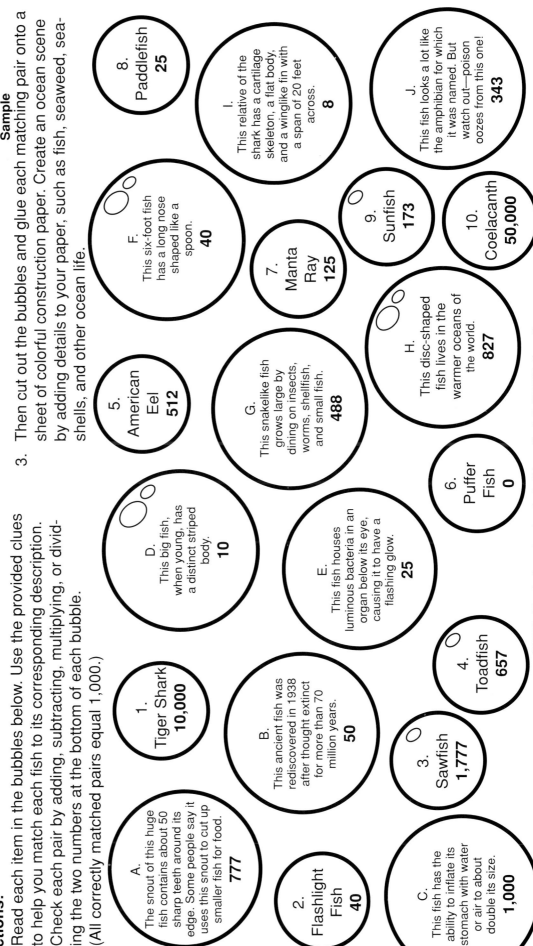

8. Paddlefish **25**

I. This relative of the shark has a cartilage skeleton, a flat body, and a winglike fin with a span of 20 feet across. **8**

J. This fish looks a lot like the amphibian for which it was named. But watch out—poison oozes from this one! **343**

F. This six-foot fish has a long nose shaped like a spoon. **40**

7. Manta Ray **125**

9. Sunfish **173**

10. Coelacanth **50,000**

H. This disc-shaped fish lives in the warmer oceans of the world. **827**

5. American Eel **512**

G. This snakelike fish grows large by dining on insects, worms, shellfish, and small fish. **488**

6. Puffer Fish **0**

D. This big fish, when young, has a distinct striped body. **10**

E. This fish houses luminous bacteria in an organ below its eye, causing it to have a flashing glow. **25**

4. Toadfish **657**

1. Tiger Shark **10,000**

B. This ancient fish was rediscovered in 1938 after thought extinct for more than 70 million years. **50**

3. Sawfish **1,777**

A. The snout of this huge fish contains about 50 sharp teeth around its edge. Some people say it uses this snout to cut up smaller fish for food. **777**

2. Flashlight Fish **40**

C. This fish has the ability to inflate its stomach with water or air to about double its size. **1,000**

Note to the teacher: Give each student one 9" x 12" sheet of light blue construction paper, scissors, glue, and markers or crayons. Also provide each student access to reference materials, if needed.

The Tropical Rain Forest

Take your students on a journey filled with rich information of the rain forest with these ready-to-go activities and reproducibles.

Background for the Teacher

- On average, tropical rain forests get between 50 and 260 inches of rain each year.
- Almost all the world's tropical rain forests lie between the Tropics of Cancer and Capricorn, about 30° north and 30° south of the equator.
- Over 50 percent of the world's plants and animals are found in rain forests.
- Only about five percent of the sunlight ever reaches the rain forest floor. Therefore, little vegetation grows there.
- Most plant nutrients found in a rain forest are in the living vegetation, not the soil; so when the rain forests are destroyed, the land is only useful for growing crops or raising cattle for a few years.
- Because many scientists believe the earth's climate is affected by the tropical rain forests' water cycles, they worry about the climatic effects of their destruction.
- Many foods, vital medicines, and other products (like wood and rubber) come from the rain forest.
- One quarter of our medicines come from rain forest plants. Yet only one percent of these plants have been thoroughly tested for their medicinal uses.
- Close to half of the world's rain forests are gone. They are being cut down for logging operations, cash crops, cattle ranches, and homes.
- It's estimated that 50 million acres of rain forests are destroyed each year.
- Because of rain forest destruction, approximately 100 species of plants and animals become extinct each day.

Classroom Rain Forest
(Research, Art)

Take your students on a rain forest field trip without stepping foot out of your classroom! To begin, make a large rain forest tree on one wall of your classroom (see the illustration below). Rumple brown bulletin board paper or brown paper bags for the bark. Then add to the branches large leaves and *lianas,* or woody vines, made from green bulletin board paper. To give your rain forest tree a three-dimensional look, make two cutouts for each leaf and vine. Staple around the edges, leaving enough room to stuff them with fiberfill (available at most craft supply stores), and then staple them closed.

Next, read to your students *Rain Forest Secrets* by Arthur Dorros (Scholastic Inc., 1999). After reading, have your class list all the different kinds of plants and animals shown or described in the book. Then pair students and give each pair a 9" x 12" sheet of white construction paper, markers or crayons, scissors, and a large index card. Assign each pair a different plant or animal from the compiled list to research. Direct the pair to draw, color, and cut out the plant or animal and then write its name and an interesting fact on the index card. For example, "Howler monkeys are known for their incredibly loud howling in the mornings, which can be heard up to two miles away." Finally, invite students to attach their finished rainforest projects among the tree's leaves and vines.

Reading About Rain Forests

The Most Beautiful Roof in the World by Kathryn Lasky (Gulliver Green, 1997)
Mysteries of the Rain Forest: 20th Century Medicine Man adapted by Elaine Pascoe (Blackbirch Press, Inc.; 1998)
Rain Forest Secrets by Arthur Dorros (Scholastic Inc., 1999)
A Rain Forest Tree (Small Worlds series) by Lorien Kite (Crabtree Publishing Company, 1999)
Welcome to the Green House by Jane Yolen (G. P. Putnam's Sons, 1997).

Bringing the Rain Forest to Life

(Dramatization, Research, Organizing Information, Descriptive Writing)

For a better understanding of the ever important layers of the rain forest, have your young thespians dramatize the role that each one plays. Begin by dividing your students into groups of four. Assign each group member a different rain forest layer: *forest floor, understory, canopy,* and *emergent layer.* Then, as you share information about each layer from the box below, have each student act out his role: each forest floor student lies down; each understory student sits, pretzel-style, and stretches one arm out to his side; each canopy student kneels with his arms spread out over the understory; and each emergent layer student stands with his arms at his sides. Next, pose the following question to students: "What might happen when one of the canopy or emergent layer trees dies?" Explain that when this happens, sunlight then reaches the lower levels, forest floor seedlings sprout up into the understory, and understory trees grow up into the canopy. Demonstrate this process by having each emergent layer student lie down on the floor, each forest floor student sit, each understory student kneel, and each canopy student stand.

Follow up the activity by distributing a copy of the organizer on page 32 to each group. Have students, in their groups, complete the activity as directed on the page. Then have students share their information with the class.

A Little About Rain Forest Layers

The first layer of the forest is the *floor.* It receives little sunlight and has a thin cover of fallen leaves. These leaves are broken down by insects and, when coupled with the humidity, can decompose within a week's time. The next layer, the *understory,* is filled with shrubs, ferns, and small trees trying to catch the limited sunlight. The third layer, the *canopy,* is an almost solid layer of leaves and branches of tall trees that support most of the abundant rain forest life. Finally, the topmost layer, the *emergent layer,* is a few tall trees that spread out high above the canopy.

Rain Forest in a Bottle

(Creating a Terrarium)

Part of what makes a rain forest unique is its soil composition and its self-sustaining water cycle. Help your students observe these elements firsthand by creating a rain forest terrarium. To complete the activity, divide your class into groups of four. Provide each group with the materials and a copy of the directions below. Guide groups in completing the activity, and then at the end of two weeks, discuss students' findings. *(The gravel and the soil show how, in the rain forest, only about four inches of fertile soil lies atop hard red clay. The blood meal, a natural fertilizer, shows how animal decomposition can benefit plant growth. The dead vegetation on the rain forest floor [the crushed leaves] is a mulch that, among other things, provides needed nutrients to living plants. The plastic wrap over the top of the bottle reproduces the humidity and the unique water cycle found in the rain forest. For further information about this water cycle, see "Plants That Make It Pour" on page 31.)*

Materials needed for each group: 1 clear, 2-liter soda bottle with the top cut off; 2 cups gravel; 2 cups potting soil; 3 green bean seeds; $1/4$ cup water; 1 handful dry leaves, crushed; 1 teaspoon blood meal (found in most hardware and garden shops); plastic wrap; 1 large rubber band

Directions:
1. Put the gravel into the bottom of the bottle.
2. Put the soil on top of the gravel.
3. Plant the green bean seeds close to the top of the soil with space between each one.
4. Pour $1/8$ cup water over the soil. Put crushed leaves on top of the soil. Sprinkle on the blood meal. Pour another $1/8$ cup water over the top.
5. Cover the bottle with plastic wrap and seal it tightly with a rubber band.
6. Record observations daily for two weeks.

A Day in the Life of a Rain Forest Animal
(Research, Organizing Information, Creative Writing, Art)

Millions of different animals make their homes in the rain forest. Have students discover what day-to-day life is like for a chosen few of these amazing creatures by writing about them—from the animals' points of view. Have each student choose a different rain forest animal to research for its habitat, physical description, behavior, diet, predators, and any other important information (such as if the animal is an endangered species). Direct the student to sort her information in a graphic organizer such as the one shown. Next, have each student use the organizer to help her write a story, from the animal's point of view, that describes a typical day in its life. Next, give each student a file folder, a variety of arts-and-craft supplies, scissors, and glue. Direct the student to use the provided supplies to illustrate her animal in its natural habitat on one side of the folder. On the other side of the folder have the student glue her organizer and the final copy of her story. Make a display of these daily-life descriptions by placing each opened file folder on a table or shelf.

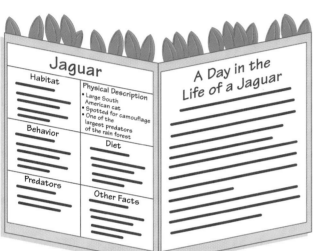

Jaguar

Habitat	Physical Description
	• Large South American cat
	• Spotted for camouflage
	• One of the largest predators of the rain forest
Behavior	Diet
Predators	Other Facts

A Day in the Life of a Jaguar

Rain Forest Resources
(Critical-Thinking Game)

Help students discover how the rain forest is rich in valuable resources that are made into products we use every day. With students' help, collect samples or pictures cut from magazines of rain forest resources such as those listed below. Display the samples and/or pictures, allowing students time to view them. Then divide students into small groups. Challenge each group to list as many uses/products as possible for each resource, with an emphasis on the unique. For example, students may identify vanilla as being used in a scented shampoo. After each group has had time to compile its list, name one of the resources and have one member from each group call out its uses/products. As like products are called out, have each group cross it off its list. If a group calls out a product that no other group has identified, have a member circle the item. Continue in the same manner until each resource is named. Afterward, identify the group with the most unique answers, and then share with students a special rain forest treat such as chocolate or gum for their efforts!

Pineapple is a topping used on pizza.

tea	cinnamon	grapefruits	coconuts	tapioca
coffee	sugar	lemons	rice	rubber
chocolate/cocoa	vanilla	limes	sesame seeds	woods such as mahogany,
black pepper	bananas	pineapples	peanuts	teak, balsa, and bamboo

Plants That Make It Pour
(Water Cycle Demonstration)

What makes the rain forest a *rain* forest? Its watery weather, of course! Share with students that thundershowers may occur in the rain forest more than 200 days each year. Further explain that up to half of the rain (and, in some parts of the forest far from the ocean, almost all of the rain) in the rain forest comes from evaporation of water from the soil and from *transpiration,* or the release of moisture through the leaves of plants. Point out to students that because of all the rain the rain forest produces for itself, some scientists fear that drought could strike areas in which rain forests have been cleared. Then show students just how this process of rain forest water recycling works. Thoroughly water a potted plant. Cover it with plastic wrap and secure the wrap around the lip of the pot with a rubber band. Then place the plant on a sunny windowsill. As students observe the water droplets building up on the inside of the plastic wrap over the next two days, ask them to tell you how it is similar to the rain forest water cycle. *(As with the plant being used in the demonstration, after the water evaporates from the rain forest's soil and plant leaves [from transpiration], it forms water droplets in the surrounding air [clouds] that slowly condense and fall back to the earth as rain. It recycles the same water over and over again.)*

A Circle of Destruction
(Demonstration)

Bring students' understanding of the effects—on plants, animals, and humans—of losing the rain forest full circle with this student-centered demonstration. Begin by sharing these startling statistics with your class: 90 rain forest tribes have been destroyed in the past century in the Amazon alone; approximately 100 species of plants and animals become extinct each day; an estimated 50 million acres are destroyed each year and if nothing is done to stop this destruction, rain forests may disappear from the earth within students' lifetimes. Next, copy each rain forest item from the list below onto the chalkboard or a sheet of chart paper. Then have students join hands and form a circle. Beginning with one student and moving in a clockwise direction, have each student, in turn, call out a different item on the list, leave the circle, and then sit back down at his desk. Instruct students remaining in the circle to close up the gap. Continue in this manner until all students are seated. Finally, guide students in seeing how the shrinking circle represented the species of plants and animals that may be lost forever if the rain forest continues to be destroyed.

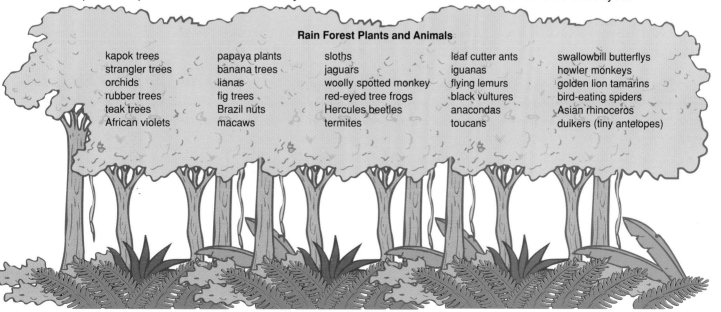

Rain Forest Plants and Animals

kapok trees	papaya plants	sloths	leaf cutter ants	swallowbill butterflys
strangler trees	banana trees	jaguars	iguanas	howler monkeys
orchids	lianas	woolly spotted monkey	flying lemurs	golden lion tamarins
rubber trees	fig trees	red-eyed tree frogs	black vultures	bird-eating spiders
teak trees	Brazil nuts	Hercules beetles	anacondas	Asian rhinoceros
African violets	macaws	termites	toucans	duikers (tiny antelopes)

Layers of Life

Each layer of the rain forest is a rich treasure trove of life. Read the headings on the organizer below. Then research each layer for the information listed. Write your information in the corresponding space on the chart. Finally, use the information to write a descriptive paragraph on the back of this sheet about life in the layers of the rain forest.

	Unique Features and Conditions	Plants Living in the Layer	Animals Living in the Layer
Emergent Layer			
Canopy			
Understory			
Forest Floor			

©2000 The Education Center, Inc. • *Investigating Science • The Earth* • TEC1734 • Key p. 48

Note to the teacher: Use with "Bringing the Rain Forest to Life" on page 29.

Name_____ *Critical thinking*

Harmful or Not?

The rain forest provides many useful products for people. What is done to obtain these products is sometimes harmful to the rain forest. Any activity that involves *deforestation* is harmful to the rain forest's survival. Deforestation is the destroying of forests by cutting down trees to clear land for farms and other reasons.

Directions: Read the activities listed on the leaves below. Decide if the activity is *harmful* or *not harmful* to the rain forest. Then cut out each leaf and glue it to the correct tree. Use reference materials for help, if needed.

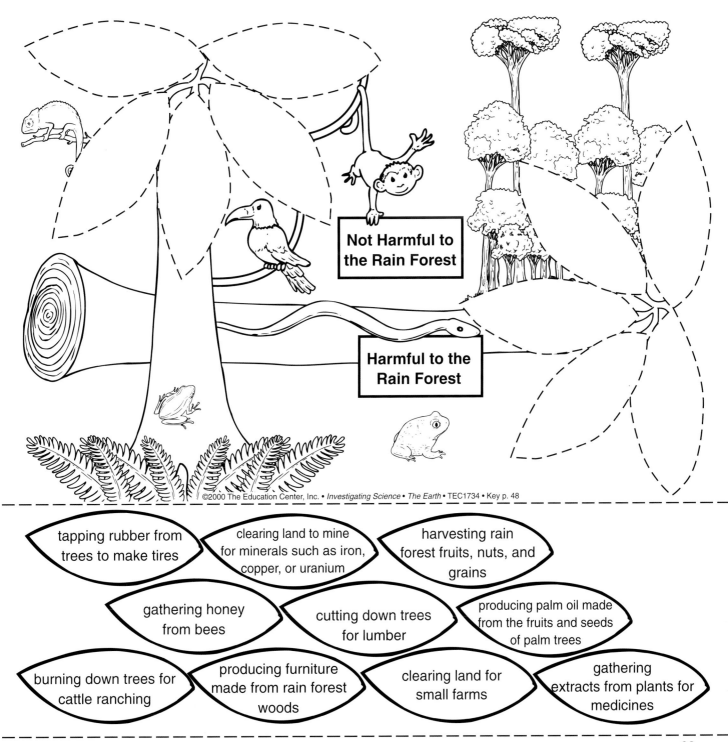

Not Harmful to the Rain Forest

Harmful to the Rain Forest

©2000 The Education Center, Inc. • *Investigating Science • The Earth* • TEC1734 • Key p. 48

tapping rubber from trees to make tires

clearing land to mine for minerals such as iron, copper, or uranium

harvesting rain forest fruits, nuts, and grains

gathering honey from bees

cutting down trees for lumber

producing palm oil made from the fruits and seeds of palm trees

burning down trees for cattle ranching

producing furniture made from rain forest woods

clearing land for small farms

gathering extracts from plants for medicines

Protecting the Environment

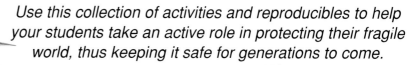

Use this collection of activities and reproducibles to help your students take an active role in protecting their fragile world, thus keeping it safe for generations to come.

Background for the Teacher

- The earth's natural environment, including its mountains, valleys, oceans, and rivers, is constantly changing. Rapid change over a short period of time could be harmful to the environment—and to the plants, animals, and people living in it.
- *Pollution* is anything not from nature that harms the environment.
- Three main types of pollution are *air, water,* and *soil* pollution.
- When pollutants combine with rainwater in clouds, *acid rain* is formed.
- Only 5% of the earth's population lives in the United States, but the United States uses 34% of the earth's energy.
- The average American produces about three pounds of trash every day.
- If all of the Styrofoam® cups that are manufactured in one day were lined up end to end, they would wrap around the planet.
- *Conservation* is the wise use of the land and its natural resources in order to prevent abuse, ruin, or disregard.
- *Preservation* is the act of preserving, or keeping intact, the land and its natural resources.
- *Reduce* means to create less waste. *Reuse* means to use the same item again or to use an old product for a new purpose. *Recycle* means to use the material of an old product to make a new product instead of throwing it away.
- Earth Day is celebrated on April 22. The first Earth Day was observed on April 22, 1970.

What are the 3 Rs?
X—Reduce, Reuse, Recycle
O—Revise, Renew, Redo

What can be dumped in a river?
X—nothing
O—trash, food, clothing

Which items can be recycled?
X—candy, juice, corn
O—glass, plastic, metal

Planet-Friendly Booklist

Common Ground: The Water, Earth, and Air We Share by Molly Bang (Scholastic Inc., 1997)

Dear Children of the Earth by Schim Schimmel (NorthWord Press, 1994)

Forests for the Future (Protecting Our Planet series) by Edward Parker (Steck-Vaughn Company, 1998)

Our Big Home: An Earth Poem by Linda Glaser (The Millbrook Press, Inc.; 2000)

Pollution and Waste (Young Discoverers series) by Rosie Harlow and Sally Morgan (Kingfisher, 1995)

A River Ran Wild by Lynne Cherry (Harcourt Brace Jovanovich, Publishers; 1992)

Tic-Tac-Toe Toward Environmental Protection
(Game)

Kick off your study of the environment with this fun fact-filled game. Ahead of time make 35–40 question cards about common environmental issues (for example, littering, recycling, clean water, etc.). Write one correct and one incorrect answer on each card; then randomly assign each answer either an "X" or an "O." In the bottom right-hand corner of each card, mark the correct answer's X or O symbol in red as shown. Next, choose nine students to be players. Have the players sit in a grid formation of three rows of three students. Provide each player with two large index cards. Have the student mark a large "X" on one and a large "O" on another. Divide the remaining students into two groups. Choose one student from each group to act as a contestant. Provide each contestant with an index card; then assign one contestant to write "X" on his card and the other contestant to write "O." Then sit with the contestants on either side of you facing the players. To play the game, select an environmental issue card and read the question to one of the contestants. Direct the contestant to select a player to answer the question. If the player answers correctly, he will hold up his "X" or "O" card to represent the contestant's symbol. If the player answers incorrectly, he doesn't hold a card up. Play continues until a contestant makes a tic-tac-toe or the game ends in a draw. To begin a new game, have the two contestants take the place of two players; then choose two new contestants from the groups.

Putting Pollution in Perspective
(Research, Making a Graphic Organizer)

Most students know that pollution harms the environment, but do they realize how many different types of pollution there are? Help your students identify the main types of pollution by having them make unique fact charts. To begin, review the definition of pollution in the background information with students. Then explain to students that there are five types of pollution: *air pollution, water pollution, soil pollution, solid waste pollution,* and *noise pollution.* Further explain that most of these pollutants come from products that many people need and want. For example, while automobiles provide the convenience of quick transportation, they create a large percentage of the world's air and noise pollution.

Pair students and provide each pair with resource materials. Direct the pair to research each type of pollution mentioned above. Next, have the pair create a pollution fact chart on a large sheet of white drawing paper, including several examples of the pollutant, an explanation of how it harms the environment (effects), and a suggestion for how to reduce it (see the example chart shown). After the pair has completed its chart, have the partners carefully *distress* the chart by crumpling the paper, tearing its edges, and smudging it with dark colors to represent the effects pollution has on our Earth. Display the charts on a bulletin board titled "We're 'Distressed' About Pollution."

by Tom and John

Pollution Chart

Type	Examples	Effects	Reduction Ideas
air pollution	• fuel exhaust • smoke	• harms plants and animals, and can damage buildings	• use cars less • develop better gas
water pollution	• sewage, oils, and toxic chemicals in the water	• can damage an animal's fur or feathers • if swallowed it can prevent an animal from breathing or even poison it	• don't dump trash in water • build safer ships to transport oil

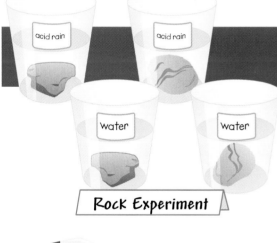

Rock Experiment

Plant Experiment

Acid Rain, Acid Rain, Go Away
(Experiment)

Here's an activity that will help your students become more aware of ways to protect the earth from one of the most serious environmental problems—acid rain. Begin by explaining to students that when pollution—in the form of the chemicals sulfur and nitrogen oxides—combines with water vapor, sunlight, and oxygen in the atmosphere, *acid rain* is formed. Further explain that when this mixture falls as rain, it can produce harmful results, such as a reduction in soil fertility, damage to trees and other plants, and the erosion of limestone or marble statues and buildings. Next, divide students into groups to observe the effects of acid rain on plants and rocks. Provide each group with the materials listed below and a copy of page 39. Instruct each group to compiete page 39 as directed. Then discuss the outcome of each group's experiments. *(Experiment results should be visible in about seven days.)*

Materials for each group:
Rock Experiment: 2 limestone and 2 marble rocks (limestone and marble chips can be found in most garden shops), 2 clear plastic cups filled ³/₄ full of water and labeled "water," 2 clear plastic cups filled ³/₄ full of vinegar and labeled "acid rain"

Plant Experiment: 2 similarly sized small plants (one labeled "water" and one labeled "acid rain"), 2 spray bottles (one filled with water and labeled "water" and the other filled with half water and half white vinegar and labeled "acid rain")

Responsible Use of Renewable Resources
(Experiment, Critical Thinking)

Clue students in to the consequences of cutting down our forests and using up other renewable resources with this critical-thinking activity. To begin, explain to students the differences between *renewable* and *nonrenewable* resources. Nonrenewable resources—such as coal, iron, and petroleum—can't be replaced once they are used. Renewable resources—such as trees, water, soil, and air—can be replaced. Next, pair students and provide each pair with the materials listed below. Have the pair put the rice in its bowl and then stand all of the pretzels upright in the rice to represent trees in a forest as shown. Then divide the pairs into two groups—reforestation foresters and deforestation foresters. Display a transparency of the "Forest Trip Script" shown. Read each step aloud. Have the students within each pair take turns "cutting down" the allotted number of trees by removing the pretzel sticks from the rice, then storing them in the condiment cup until the end of the activity. After each pair completes a trip into the forest, have the partners sort their remaining trees into groups of five as you distribute one pretzel for every group of five trees remaining. Allow the pairs to continue making trips into the forests until the deforestation foresters have cut down all of their trees. *(The reforestation foresters will always keep 30 trees in their forests due to responsible cutting, whereas the deforestation foresters will cut down all of the trees in their forests because of irresponsible cutting.)* Finally, discuss with the students the effects of cutting down too many trees while they enjoy eating their pretzels.

Materials for each pair: 1–1½ c. rice, 30 pretzel sticks, large Styrofoam® bowl, condiment cup

---

Forest Trip Script

Reforestation Forest

Trip One:
1. The forest has 30 trees.
2. Cut down five.
3. Twenty-five trees are left in the forest—five groups of five.
4. Plant five new trees.

Trip Two:
1. The forest has 30 trees.
2. Cut down five.
3. Twenty-five trees are left in the forest—five groups of five.
4. Plant five new trees.

Deforestation Forest

Trip One:
1. The forest has 30 trees.
2. Cut down ten.
3. Twenty trees are left in the forest—four groups of five.
4. Plant four new trees.

Trip Two:
1. The forest has 24 trees.
2. Cut down ten.
3. Fourteen trees are left in the forest—two groups of five, plus four extra trees.
4. Plant two new trees.

Trip Three:
1. The forest has 16 trees.
2. Cut down ten.
3. Six trees are left in the forest—one group of five, plus one extra tree.
4. Plant one new tree.

Trip Four:
1. The forest has seven trees.
2. Cut down seven.
3. There are no trees left in the forest.

©2000 The Education Center, Inc. • *Investigating Science • The Earth • TEC1734*

Windows on the World
(Research, Writing)

Use this activity to help your students understand the importance of protecting our environment to ensure the survival of living things. Begin by explaining to students that since the late 1800s humans have become more concerned with protecting animals from extinction. Further explain that we now know that there is a "web of life" that connects all of the species on the earth. In this web, if large numbers of a species disappear, the survival of other animals in the web is threatened. Many people, called *conservationists,* are working to protect the habitats of endangered animals around the world. Next, assign each child an endangered animal from the list below. Have each student use encyclopedias, books, and other resource materials to research her endangered animal—its habitat, how it became threatened, and actions that are being taken to protect it. Then provide the student with the materials listed and a copy of the directions shown. Direct the student to create a window showing her animal's world (see the example shown). Display the windows around the room so that every student can better see how to protect the earth's environment and all of the animals that live in it.

Materials for each student: 2 different light-colored sheets of 12" x 18" construction paper, masking tape, scissors, glue, markers or crayons

Directions:
1. Fold one sheet of paper in half vertically, then in half horizontally to make two fold lines on the paper.
2. Place masking tape over both fold lines to make four sections on the paper that look like windows.
3. Use the other sheet of paper to decorate a curtain around the window as shown.
4. In the first windowpane, write the name of your animal and add a picture of it.
5. Fill in each remaining windowpane with information about your endangered animal.

Endangered Animals

bridled nailtail wallaby	tiger	whooping crane
mountain gorilla	snow leopard	woolly spider monkey
aye-aye	wild yak	black-footed ferret
black rhinoceros	Pyrenean ibex	pileated gibbon
Indus River dolphin	California condor	orangutan
black colobus	ivory-billed woodpecker	Central Asian cobra
addax	green sea turtle	Przewalski's horse
Indian elephant	Argentine pampas deer	giant panda

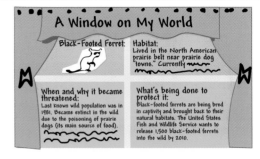

Classroom Consciousness
(Planning a Recycling Program)

Most students are aware of the need to recycle and use less trash, but they might not be personally involved in a recycling program. Have students witness firsthand how raising recycling awareness can change their environment. To begin, prepare and display a transparency of the facts below to discuss with students. Next, divide the students into small groups. Assign each group one of the three Rs: reduce, reuse, or recycle. Provide each group with a copy of the directions shown, poster board, lined writing paper, and markers and crayons. Direct each group to follow the directions and work cooperatively to create a conservation plan for reducing, reusing, or recycling materials found in the classroom. Set aside time for each group to present its plan to the class. Have the students vote on the top three plans. Then submit the plans to your principal as opportunities to implement schoolwide conservation programs.

Group Three's Plan for Reducing Paper Use

Background: After keeping track of the number of lined sheets of paper used in one day, we know that our class uses about 40 sheets in one day.

The Plan: To reduce the amount of paper, our class will use both sides of the paper.

Predicted Outcome: We think that if our plan is followed, we will use five fewer lined sheets of paper each day.

Letting People Know About the Plan: We will make posters reminding people to use both sides of the paper. We will display the posters near the paper trays and the trash cans.

Results: After following our plan for one day, we reduced the amount of paper we used by seven sheets.

Directions for each group:

1. Brainstorm a list of materials or energies you can reduce, reuse, or recycle in the classroom. (For example, use less air conditioning, reuse construction paper scraps, recycle plastic wrappers.)
2. Choose one item from your list.
3. Create a plan similar to the one your teacher shared with you on a sheet of poster board. Include information about how your item is currently used; a plan for reducing, reusing, or recycling your item; a prediction of how your plan will affect the item's use; a description of how you will put your plan into effect; and information about how your plan affected the item's use.

Fast Facts

Fact: Two hundred fifty million pounds of plastic per year has been kept out of the waste system by *reducing* the weight of a two-liter plastic soft drink bottle from 68 grams to 51 grams.

We can further reduce the amount of waste we create by designing, manufacturing, buying, and using materials in more conservative ways.

Fact: There are more than 6,000 reuse centers around the country. They range from small-scale local programs in schools to fully funded organizations like Goodwill Industries® and The Salvation Army®.

Reusing items can help stop wastefulness. This is because an item that is reused is delayed or sometimes even prevented from entering the waste collection and disposal system.

Fact: Today the United States recycles 28% of its waste. That is double the amount recycled 15 years ago.

Recycling involves three main steps: (1) collecting recyclable materials, such as paper, glass, metal, and plastic, (2) cleaning and separating the items, and (3) then processing them into new or different materials. For a recycling program to work, people need to make recycling part of their everyday routine.

Half-Gallon Container

Used to hold milk or juice

Mail Storer: Can be used to hold important items before they're mailed.

Recycling Share Fair
(Creative Problem Solving)

Here's an activity that's sure to have your students believing the familiar saying "One man's trash is another man's treasure!" Direct each student to bring an empty, cleaned item from home that was going to be thrown away (for example, a large plastic soda bottle, an empty powder-detergent box, cardboard packaging, a glass jar, or a plastic container). Provide each student with an index card. Have the child write on one side of the card the name of the item he brought in along with a description of its use. Place all the items at the front of the room with their index-card explanations. Then have each student select an item that is not his own. Direct the student to read the index card and then think of a way to create another use for the item. Have a collection of arts-and-crafts supplies on hand for each student to use to re-create his object. Finally, have the student write the name of his new creation and a description of its use on the other side of the index card. Set aside time for students to share their recycled creations with their classmates. If desired, further extend this activity by giving each student a copy of page 40 to complete as directed.

How Much Is Too Much?
(Critical Thinking, Letter Writing)

We all enjoy gifts wrapped in pretty packaging, but not when that packaging contributes unnecessary trash to our landfills and recycling centers! Help your students become Earth-conscious consumers with this letter-writing activity. To begin, explain to students that manufacturers sometimes use excessive packaging to make their products more attractive. For example, a box of chocolates may have five or six layers of packaging. Further explain that this excess packaging creates unnecessary trash—up to one-third of the garbage in a landfill is made up of discarded packaging. Ask students to bring examples of different types of packaging to class, such as from toys, perfumes, foods, and mailed items. Guide each student in writing the name of her packaged product along with the name and address of its manufacturer on an index card as shown. (If the manufacturer's address isn't on the package, use an Internet search engine to locate an address for the company.)

Collect the packaging samples; then, together with students, group the packaging into two groups: *excessive* packaging and *necessary* packaging. Then pair students and provide each pair with a different packaging sample from each group. Have the pairs discuss the packaging in relation to the products. Then have the partners write two letters: one to the manufacturer of the excessive packaging, asking the company to use less packaging and providing a suggestion for ways to do so, and the other to the manufacturer of the necessary packaging, congratulating the company on being environmentally friendly. Mail the letters, and then thank your students for becoming more consumer savvy about product packaging.

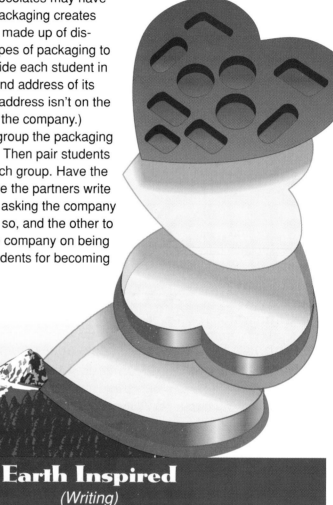

Earth Inspired
(Writing)

Earth, Earth,
My friend the Earth,
You give me a home,

The Gazette

This Earth Day have your students present the earth with gifts from their hearts. A few days before Earth Day, explain to students the origins of the day. The first Earth Day was organized by former Senator Gaylord Nelson on April 22, 1970. Senator Nelson wanted people across the country to learn what was happening to the earth's environment. He also wanted to give people a chance to share their ideas for helping the earth. More than 20 million people across the United States participated. Further explain that today, Earth Day is celebrated by people around the planet. Next, have each student make a list of ten things she wishes she could change or create to keep the earth healthy. Direct her to choose one item from her list to give the earth as a gift. Have the student write a story, poem, letter, skit, invitation, or song explaining how she would like to help the earth. Have each student place her "gift of words" in a sealed envelope. Collect the envelopes and place them inside a shoebox. Have a student volunteer wrap the box with newspaper or recycled brown paper, tie a yarn bow around it, and place it at the front of the room. On Earth Day, set aside time to open the earth's present and read each student's gift aloud. To further extend this idea, provide each student with a copy of page 41 to complete as directed.

Understanding Acid Rain

Purpose: Determine the effects of acid rain on different types of rocks.

Hypothesis: What do you think will happen when the rocks are exposed to plain water and to acid?

Materials/Procedure: Place each of the two types of rocks in the liquids—one in the cup of vinegar and one in water. List the types of rocks on the chart below.

Observation: Observe the rocks after 24 hours and again after seven days. Describe any changes in the rocks (or in the liquids) on the chart below.

Kind of Rock	In Water		In Acid (Vinegar)	
	After 24 Hours	After 7 Days	After 24 Hours	After 7 Days

Conclusion: _____

Purpose: Determine the effects of acid rain on plants.

Hypothesis: What do you think will happen to the plant spritzed with acid compared to the plant spritzed with water?

Materials/Procedure: Daily, for seven days, use the spray bottle marked "water" to spritz the plant marked "water" and the spray bottle marked "acid rain" to spritz the plant marked "acid rain."

Observation: Observe the plants after 24 hours and again after seven days. Describe any changes in the plants, especially differences in size, number of leaves, color, or appearance. Also sketch a picture of each plant after 24 hours and then after seven days in the space provided.

Plant	After 24 Hours	Picture	After 7 Days	Picture
Spritzed With Water				
Spritzed With "Acid Rain"				

Conclusion: _____

Note to the teacher: Use with "Acid Rain, Acid Rain, Go Away" on page 35.

What a Waste!

Every day Americans throw away about 907,000 metric tons of solid waste. That's about 9 pounds of trash per person! Follow the directions below to find out what types of trash get thrown out the most.

Directions: Look at the pie chart and the key below. Write each trash amount (percentage) in the correct pie piece on the chart. Color the key; then color each pie piece to match. Finally, use the chart to answer the questions below.

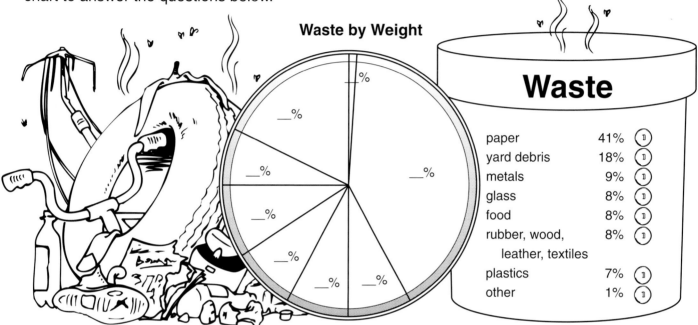

Waste by Weight

Waste		
paper	41%	
yard debris	18%	
metals	9%	
glass	8%	
food	8%	
rubber, wood, leather, textiles	8%	
plastics	7%	
other	1%	

1. Nearly half of all the waste shown on the graph belongs in which category? _____
    List five types of materials that could be found in this category and could be recycled. _____
    _____

2. What percentage of the total waste is not included in the paper category? _____

3. The second largest category contains items that are usually found in nature. List five items
    that might be found in this category. _____
    _____

4. How much more of the total waste comes from yard debris than from rubber, wood, leather,
    and textiles? _____

5. Twenty-four percent of the waste shown on the graph comes from three categories, each with
    the same amount of waste. What are the categories? List an example of two items that might
    be thrown away in each of these categories. _____
    _____

6. Some categories on the graph represent common recyclable materials that are often thrown
    away. What are these categories and what is their total percentage? _____
    _____

Bonus Box: On the back of this page, make a list of 25 items that you throw away at home. Divide these items into the categories above. Then make a bar graph estimating the amount of trash you throw away in each category.

Gold Medal Reactions

On April 22, 1970, the first Earth Day was celebrated. Sponsors of the event hoped that each person would do his or her part at home, at work, and in the community to protect the earth. By focusing on how pollution and other environmental risks affect people no matter where they live, Earth Day encourages people all over the world to "Give Earth a Chance."

Directions: Read each situation below. Then write how you would react to each situation on the lines provided.

Situation	Reaction
1. Someone throws trash from a car window.	
2. A neighbor plays loud music late into the night.	
3. A business dumps chemicals into the city lake.	
4. A girl spray-paints a message on a tree.	
5. A government allows a large section of a forest to be burnt down.	
6. A developer builds a new superstore in a wilderness area.	
7. A car company makes a huge car that releases chemicals into the air.	

Name _____ *Critical thinking*

Did you know that every time you take a shower or pour a glass of lemonade you are using the same water that the dinosaurs used? For millions of years, our water has recycled and cleansed itself through a process called the *hydrologic cycle.* Today, however, because of pollution, pure water is seldom found in nature. This is because water is an excellent *solvent*—other substances dissolve easily into it. This means that as water travels up into plants, it carries with it not only minerals and nutrients, but harmful dissolved chemicals that pollute the water and endanger plants, animals, and people.

Be Water Wise!

Directions: Read each statement below. Then add to each statement by writing in actions that you should take to conserve our precious water resources.

Every Drop Counts!

1. Use only as much water as needed.
    So I should _____

    _____

2. A deep bathtub can hold up to 26 gallons of water.
    So I should _____

    _____

3. A slowly dripping faucet can waste 3 gallons of water per day.
    So I should _____

    _____

4. Water used with detergents and other cleaning products must be treated.
    So I should _____

    _____

5. Oil, paint, and other chemicals need to be dumped according to special instructions.
    So I should _____

    _____

6. Keeping an eye on the water supply is everyone's job.
    So I should _____

    _____

7. There are other reasons for using water wisely besides preventing water pollution.
    So I should _____

    _____

Bonus Box: Pretend you have a tall glass of water. Imagine all of the different places the water could have been. On the back of this page, write and illustrate a short "history" about your water.

©2000 The Education Center, Inc. • *Investigating Science • The Earth* • TEC1734 • Key p. 48

Eye on the Environment

Hot Topic

(picture)

_____
(title)

_____

_____

_____

_____

_____

_____

_____

_____

_____

Reported by _____

Fast Facts

• _____
_____

• _____
_____

• _____
_____

• _____
_____

• _____
_____

• _____
_____

• _____
_____

Sources

©2000 The Education Center, Inc. • *Investigating Science* • *The Earth* • TEC1734

Note to the teacher: Assign each student a different environmental topic being studied (such as one from the background information on page 34). Have the student use appropriate resource materials to research the topic. Then have the student create an informational magazine page about his topic by completing each section above. Combine the students' research pages into a class magazine titled "Our Eyes Are on the Environment."

Earthquakes and Volcanoes

Get your students movin' and shakin' using the following creative activities and reproducibles.

Background for the Teacher

- The earth has four main layers. From the inside out, they are the *core, outer core, mantle,* and *crust.*
- The mantle is partly solid and partly melted rock called *magma.*
- The crust varies in thickness from 25 miles (continental crust) to about 5 miles (oceanic crust).
- The crust and the topmost portion of the mantle make up the earth's *plates.* Plates are large portions of the earth's surface which move as units.
- Volcanoes are produced when molten material, *lava,* erupts through any place on the earth's surface.
- Earthquakes are a sudden, violent shaking of the earth caused by a shifting of the earth's crust. An earthquake's energy builds up from within the earth and is released through weak points in the crust called *faults.*
- An earthquake's strength, or *magnitude,* is recorded by a seismograph. The Richter scale is used to show the scale of this magnitude.
- Both earthquakes and volcanoes can result in loss of plant, animal, and human life; damage to property; and disasters such as landslides, floods, and fires.

Earthshaking Books

Earthquakes by Sally M. Walker (Carolrhoda Books, Inc.; 1996)

Shake, Rattle, and Roll: The World's Most Amazing Volcanoes, Earthquakes, and Other Forces (Spencer Christian's World of Wonders series) by Spencer Christian and Antonia Felix (John Wiley & Sons, Inc.; 1997)

Volcano: The Violent Earth by John Dudman (Thomson Learning, 1993)

Volcano & Earthquake (Dorling Kindersley Eyewitness Books) by Susanna Van Rose (Alfred A. Knopf, Inc.; 1992)

Volcanologist's View
(Research, Writing, Art)

Send your budding volcanologists on a research expedition that results in the creation of a desktop reference guide. Remind students how volcanoes are produced (see the Background for the Teacher on this page). Point out that although volcanoes can be many shapes and sizes, there are three basic forms: *composite, cinder,* and *shield.* The *viscosity* (stickiness) of a volcano's lava determines what shape it will take. (See below for more information.) Next, provide each student access to appropriate reference materials. Direct the student to research each type of basic volcano formation to discover how it is formed, the materials from which it is made, and its unique features. Then guide students through the steps below to create their own desktop reference guides. If desired, laminate students' guides for durability.

- Composite Volcano—alternating layers of ash and thick lava create a tall, steep-sided mountain
- Cinder Cone—a smaller volcano made of lava, ash, and rock
- Shield Volcano—forms when thin, runny lava flows over a wide area

Materials for each student: one 9" x 12" sheet of white construction paper, crayons, scissors

Steps:

1. Fold the construction paper in half lengthwise. Then fold it in thirds as shown. (Figure 1)
2. Open the folded paper to show three equal-sized sections. Then cut along each vertical fold line on the top flap of the paper. (Figure 2)
3. Taking care not to cut the fold completely, cut the top fold of each section to resemble one type of volcano—composite, cinder, and shield. (Figure 3)
4. Write the name of the volcano on its matching outside section. Then draw and color a labeled diagram including its size, shape, and unique features (such as its vents and magma chamber).
5. On the inside flap of each volcano's section, briefly explain its formation and give a specific example of a volcano of its type.
6. Fanfold the guide so it will stand on your desk.

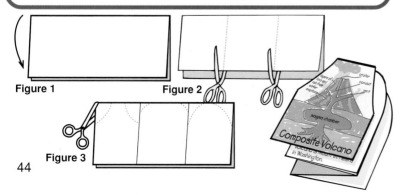

Figure 1   **Figure 2**

Figure 3

Erupting Word Problems
(Reading, Math, Critical Thinking)

Wonderful word problems will erupt from your students with this motivating math activity! Give each pair of students a copy of the story below, a sentence strip, and crayons or markers. Read the story aloud and then discuss the story events, pointing out the mathematical details. (For more information, share the story *Hill of Fire* by Thomas P. Lewis, HarperCollins Publishers, 1971.) Then have the pair use the numerical facts in the story to write and illustrate a word problem. Direct the pair to write the problem on the front of its strip and the solution on the back. Collect students' strips, displaying one at the beginning of science class each day. Have the authors of the problem read it aloud; then have each remaining student solve the problem on a piece of paper or in her science journal. At the end of the class, have the authors explain the problem's solution to the class as each student checks her work.

El Monstruo: The Monster of Paricutín, Mexico

What could have happened to turn an ordinary day for a boy on a Mexican farm into an *extraordinary* day? Cresencio Pulido could tell you. On February 20, 1943, young Cresencio tended the family sheep while his father plowed a nearby cornfield. Suddenly, with a deep rumbling noise and a loud CRACK, the earth split open. Plumes of smoke shot out of this fissure and into the air. "Run!" screamed the farmer. Then, with a loud HISS, red-hot lava spewed from the earth as the boy and his father raced to warn the people in the nearby village. The villagers watched in terror as the sky was filled with lava and fiery ash.

By the end of the first day, a volcano of lava and ash grew to about 25 feet. By the second day, the volcano was nearly 164 feet, and by the end of the first week, the volcano reached 460 feet. Within a year, the volcano was 1,100 feet, and the people had named it "El Monstruo" *(the monster)*. The whole village of Paricutín was destroyed or damaged—all except for a lone church. The volcano continued to erupt until 1952, and today the volcano reaches a height of 1,350 feet.

What was the average growth of the volcano each day of the first week?

Answer: 65.7 feet each day

Eyewitness Earthquake Accounts
(Creative Writing)

Turn your students into news reporters who share "a firsthand look" at the damage that earthquakes can cause. Share with students the background information about earthquakes on page 44. Then copy the Mercalli scale, shown below, on a transparency or a chalkboard. Share with students that this scale was invented in 1902 (and modified in 1931) as a method of describing the intensity of *damage* caused by an earthquake. Discuss each level of the scale with students, pointing out the increasing damage with each new level.

Next, pair students and assign each pair a different level on the scale. Also, designate one student in the pair to play the role of news reporter and the other the role of earthquake eyewitness. Direct each pair to write an interview dialogue describing a fictitious earthquake, including where and when the earthquake occurred, who was involved, what happened and what were the effects (using information from the scale), and why or how it happened. When the dialogues are complete, present a "talk show" in which each pair performs its interview for the class.

Modified Mercalli Intensity Scale

I Shaking not felt by people

II Shaking only felt by some people; some lightweight hanging objects swing

III Felt indoors by more people; cars rock

IV Felt indoors by many people; dishes, windows, and doors rattle; walls creak

V Felt indoors by most everyone; dishes and windows break; small objects move; small trees and shrubs shake

VI Felt by all; people frightened; books and other objects fall off shelves; dishes and windows break

VII Difficult to stand; loose bricks and plaster fall; furniture breaks; waves appear on ponds

VIII Difficult to steer cars; heavy furniture overturned; walls, chimneys and statues fall; buildings damaged; tree branches break

IX General panic arises; animals confused; underground pipes break; serious damage to buildings

X Most buildings destroyed; water thrown out of rivers; landslides occur; ground is badly cracked and railroad tracks bent

XI Few buildings remain standing; underground pipes destroyed; wide cracks in ground

XII Damage total; waves visible on the ground surface; objects thrown into the air; river courses moved

Volcanic Vocabulary

Don't you just "lava" good volcano joke? Read the vocabulary words and the clues below. Use a vocabulary word to complete each clue. Then match a letter to each numbered blank to learn the answer to the riddle.

Word Bank

upward	dormant	crust	shield	Mount St. Helens
magma	Hawaii	ash	core	volcanologist
crack	composite	mantle	molten	Washington
erupt	cinder			

1. Like an apple, the earth's __ __ __ __ is its innermost layer.

                                3

2. Two other Earth layers are the __ __ __ __ __ and the __ __ __ __ __ .

                                       15   1

3. The mantle has pockets of __ __ __ __ __ __ (melted) rock called __ __ __ __ __ .

                                   13   10

4. Magma is lighter than the surrounding rocks in the mantle so it moves __ __ __ __ __ __

                                                                                               17

toward the surface, or crust.

5. If magma reaches the surface, it may __ __ __ __ __ through a *fissure,* or __ __ __ __ __ ,

                                                               4   7

in the earth's surface.

6. Volcanoes may be __ __ __ __ __ __ __ for many years and then suddenly explode.

                                   11

7. On May 18, 1980, __ __ __ __ __ __ __ . __ __ __ __ __ __ , a dormant volcano in

                                                                               2

__ __ __ __ __ __ __ __ __ __ state, erupted for the first time in 123 years.

                                   8

8. When the volcano "blew its top," millions of tons of __ __ __ filled the air.

                                                                  14

9. Mauna Loa in __ __ __ __ __ __ is a __ __ __ __ __ __ volcano. It was formed by steady

                          9   5

flowing lava from small vents.

10. __ __ __ __ __ __ cones form when volcanoes erupt suddenly, throwing ash, lava, and rocks

                               12

into the air.

11. __ __ __ __ __ __ __ __ cones are made by repeated eruptions producing layers of ash,

                                         6

cinder, and lava.

12. A __ __ __ __ __ __ __ __ __ __ __ __ __ is a scientist who studies volcanoes.

                  16

Riddle Time! What time was it when Mount St. Helens erupted?

It was time __ __ __ __ __ __ __ , __ __ __ __ __ __ , and __ __ __ __ !

                 6 11   1 9 14 7 2   17 10 4 13 15 12   3 8 16 5

Earthquake Danger Zones

Do you ever wonder if you are in danger of experiencing an earthquake? The U.S. Geological Survey has identified five regions, or zones, that tell the strengths of earthquakes that can be expected. The zones range from 0 to 4, with 0 being the safest areas and 4 being the most dangerous.

Directions: Lightly color each box in the key below a different color. Then color the earthquake zones on the map according to your key. Finally, use the map to help you answer the questions that follow.

United States Map

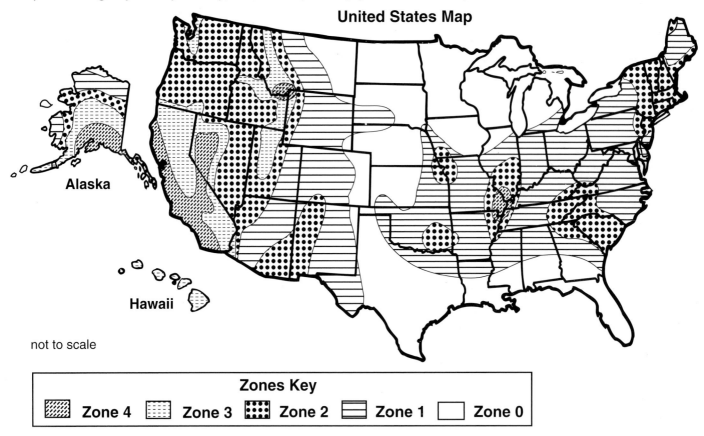

Alaska

Hawaii

not to scale

Zones Key

Zone 4   Zone 3   Zone 2   Zone 1   Zone 0

1. Name at least two states that will probably not experience an earthquake. _____

   _____

2. How many states fall into the Zone 1 risk area? _____

3. Name three states with a Zone 2 risk. _____

4. Name the states with a Zone 3 risk. _____

   _____

5. How many states are likely to experience Zone 4 strength earthquakes? _____

   Name the states. _____

6. Are the west or east coast states more at risk for strong earthquakes? _____

   In which zones do these areas fall? _____

7. How many states are in more than one zone? _____

8. Is your state at risk for an earthquake? _____ In which zone does your state fall? _____

Bonus Box: Research the name of the fault that lies off the coast of California. How does this affect the risk of experiencing a severe earthquake?

Answer Keys

Page 10
Students' answers may vary but should include the following:
1. Patches of white, green, or black material started to form on the foods. The patches look soft and cottony.
2. Decomposers were in the air inside the jar. Another way decomposers could have gotten into the jar is by water, especially if any of the food items had been washed in water before they were placed in the jar.
3. More decomposition will probably take place during that time.

Bonus Box answer: Fleming noticed that a green mold growing in a culture plate in his lab had killed the bacteria around it. This led to the discovery and development of the lifesaving antibiotic known as *penicillin.*

Page 11
Students' answers will vary based on the test items chosen.
1. Biodegradable items such as paper, cloth, an apple slice, a craft stick, hard candy, a cracker or a piece of bread, and cake would eventually decay when placed in soil. Any of these items could be included in a decomposer's diet. The wooden part of a pencil could also be included in a decomposer's diet, but not its eraser, lead, or metal band. The paper part of a disposable diaper could also be included in the diet, but not its plastic liner.
2. Nonbiodegradable items such as Styrofoam®, a small plastic toy, a disposable pen, a paper clip, a pencil (everything but the wood), a plastic grocery bag square, and a disposable diaper square do not decay easily and remain unchanged for years in landfills. These items would not be included in a decomposer's diet.

Page 17

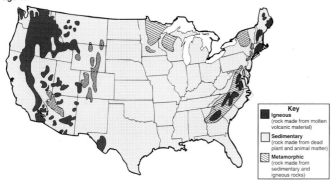

Key
- **Igneous** (rock made from molten volcanic material)
- **Sedimentary** (rock made from dead plant and animal matter)
- **Metamorphic** (rock made from sedimentary and igneous rocks)

Page 26
The Shark
- is a fish with a skeleton made of cartilage
- is covered with hard, sharp scales called *denticles*
- ranges from about six inches to 49 feet in length
- breathes through five to seven gill slits on each side
- has a vertical *caudal,* or tail, fin, which moves from side to side to propel it through the water
- is in most cases *cold-blooded,* so its body temperature changes with the surrounding water temperature
- has keen senses—sight, hearing, and smell—and can detect vibrations from great distances
- has several rows of sharp teeth, which are easily replaced when lost
- sometimes gathers with others of its kind in a feeding frenzy
- sometimes attacks people and at other times leaves them alone

The Dolphin
- is, like other whales, a mammal
- has skin that is sleek, smooth, and rubbery to the touch
- ranges from about four to nine feet in length
- breathes air through lungs and a blowhole at the top of its head
- has a horizontal *caudal,* or tail, fin, which moves up and down to propel it through the water
- is *warm-blooded,* so it maintains a constant body temperature
- is extremely vocal, making rapid clicking noises to use as a form of sonar and high-pitched whistles to communicate
- exhibits a high level of intelligence and can be trained to do tricks
- often travels in groups called *herds*
- is a playful, sociable creature that has even been credited for saving drowning swimmers

Page 27
1. D; 10,000 ÷ 10
2. E; 40 x 25
3. A; 1,777 – 777
4. J; 657 + 343
5. G; 512 + 488
6. C; 0 + 1,000
7. I; 125 x 8
8. F; 25 x 40
9. H; 173 + 827
10. B; 50,000 ÷ 50

Page 32
Students' answers will vary. Possible answers include the following:

Emergent Layer
Features and Conditions:
- A few giant trees towering over the canopy
Plants:
- Trees of all kinds of great height (over 200 feet)
Animals:
- Eagles

Canopy
Features and Conditions:
- Includes tall trees that are close together, making what looks like a carpet of green
- Branches and leaves only at the top of trees
- Most abundant life at this level
- Blocks most of the sunlight from lower levels
Plants:
- Trees of all kinds (100–200 feet), orchids, passion vines, bromeliads, mosses, algaes, woody vines
Animals:
- Harpy eagles, parrots, hornbills, toucans, macaws, hummingbirds, howler monkeys, sloths, squirrels, fruit bats, lizards, snakes, frogs, katydids, butterflies

Page 32 (Continued)
Understory
Features and Conditions:
- Includes shorter trees and shrubs that strive to find sunlight
- Scarce light
- Humid
Plants:
- All kinds of trees (less than 100 feet), including palms and tree ferns, lianas, orchids
Animals:
- Jaguars, ocelots, tamarins, chimpanzees, flying lemurs, opossums, bushbabies, toucans, birds of paradise, anteaters, snakes, frogs

Forest Floor
Features and Conditions:
- Receives very little light
- Decomposing leaf litter
- Humid, damp
- Not very rich soil, most nutrients in the vegetation
- Easy to walk on, not much growing because of little light
Plants:
- Fungi, rafflesia, moss
Animals:
- Elephants, okapis, tapirs, jaguars, ocelots, margays, porcupines, peacocks, pheasants, spiders, snails, beetles, ants, millipedes, termites

Page 33
Not Harmful to the Rain Forest
- tapping rubber from trees to make tires
- harvesting rain forest fruits, nuts, and grains
- producing palm oil made from the fruits and seeds of palm trees
- gathering extracts from plants for medicines
- gathering honey from bees

Harmful to the Rain Forest
- cutting down trees for lumber
- clearing land to mine for minerals such as iron, copper, or uranium
- burning down trees for cattle ranching
- producing furniture made from rain forest woods
- clearing land for small farms

Page 39
Rock Experiment:
Air bubbles may be seen on all of the rocks for the first day or two because air can become trapped in porous rocks. After seven days, students should observe a fine powder on the bottom of the cups containing vinegar and limestone or marble rocks. Bubbles may be seen on the limestone and marble rocks after seven days as well.

Plant Experiment:
The plants spritzed with vinegar should turn yellow, shrivel up, and possibly even die.

Page 40
1. Paper. Items in students' lists may vary.
2. 59%.
3. Items in students' lists may vary.
4. 10% more.
5. Glass; food; and rubber, wood, leather, textiles. Items in students' lists may vary.
6. Paper, metals, glass, and plastics; 65%.

Page 42
Students' answers may vary. Possible answers include the following:
1. So I should turn off the faucet when I am brushing my teeth.
2. So I should take a shower instead of a bath or not fill the tub up all the way.
3. So I should make sure all of the faucets are turned off tightly. I should never leave a faucet running.
4. So I should use detergents and other cleaning products sparingly. I should make sure the cleaning products are "environmentally friendly."
5. So I should contact my local authorities to find out where and how to dump harmful chemicals. I should never dump harmful chemicals down the drain or in the toilet.
6. So I should contact local authorities if I encounter signs of water pollution or if I see someone dumping waste into my local stream or river.
7. So I should educate myself on other reasons for using water wisely, such as keeping water bills down and ensuring there is enough water in the supply in the event of a drought.

Page 46
1. core
2. mantle, crust
3. molten, magma
4. upward
5. erupt, crack
6. dormant
7. Mount St. Helens, Washington
8. ash
9. Hawaii, shield
10. cinder
11. composite
12. volcanologist

Riddle answer: It was time to shake, rattle, and roll!

Page 47
1. Students' answers will vary: Florida, Minnesota, North Dakota, Wisconsin
2. 34.
3. Students' answers will vary: Alaska, Arizona, Arkansas, Colorado, Connecticut, Georgia, Idaho, Illinois, Indiana, Iowa, Kansas, Kentucky, Maine, Massachusetts, Mississippi, Missouri, Montana, Nebraska, Nevada, New Hampshire, New Jersey, New Mexico, New York, North Carolina, Oklahoma, Oregon, Pennsylvania, Rhode Island, South Carolina, Tennessee, Utah, Vermont, Virginia, Washington, West Virginia, Wyoming
4. Alaska, Arizona, California, Hawaii, Idaho, Montana, Nevada, Oregon, Utah, Washington, Wyoming.
5. 11: Alaska, Arkansas, California, Idaho, Illinois, Kentucky, Missouri, Montana, Nevada, Tennessee, Wyoming.
6. The west coast states. Zones 2, 3, and 4.
7. 35.
8. Students' answers will vary.

Bonus Box answer: San Andreas Fault. Most earthquakes occur along fault lines.